HALEY'S
COMMENTS

A View of Life From Across the Street

To Buddy Villines
Best wishes for
a happy life
Tom Haley
Christmas
1992

GUILDCRAFT OF INDIANA

HALEY'S
COMMENTS

A View of Life From Across the Street

Tom Haley

~ GUILDCRAFT OF INDIANA ~

The material contained in this book were previously published in *The
Benton Courier*, Benton, Arkansas, and is reproduced by permission.

Printed in the United States of America

ISBN 1-880365-01-4 (pbk.) : $12.95

First Edition, 1991
Second Edition, 1992

Cover design by Dan Coston
Photo by Philip A. Felton

~ GUILDCRAFT of INDIANA~

To my wife,

AMANDA

for her encouragement, love and understanding

Contents

Life in Texarkana ~

Life in the South ~

Life Goes On ~

Introduction

I was leaning over the sink, with saltshaker in hand, eating a whole tomato and gazing out of the kitchen window when I decided that I had to do this.

I had never written an introduction before. I was flattered that Tom asked me, but how do you introduce someone like Tom.

In a generation where writers are fixated on "quirky characters", how do you introduce someone who makes every day and every situation seem extraordinary. He is a genuinely quirky character if I have ever met one.

When Tom joined the staff of *The Benton Courier* in late 1988, I wondered why he was there. He was no hot young journalism student just out of school. He was former Methodist preacher, for heaven's sakes. But he was quick on the uptake and his rapport with folks in our semi-rural setting gave him an edge as a reporter and feature writer.

Later, when he came up with the idea of doing a column for the editorial page I thought: "uh-oh." I had seen this in the movies. Another would-be writer tries to get his foot in the door as a journalist (the more upscale sounding word for "newswriter"). The same journalist finds fame, semi-fortune and a reason to go on writing by publishing his/her thoughts on the world around them.

In this job you see egos blossom like a peach in the summer heat. Many become overripe. To many people, the mere possession of a pencil, the mailing address of the local paper and a postage stamp are a guarantee of access to the fellowship of literary fame. If you don't believe me, just read some of the letters to the editor of your local paper.

Even worse, there is a tendency in many newswriters to assume that their news-reading public will gladly follow them when they become carried away by their personal muse. Inspiration gets confused with indulgence. It's a dangerous trap that some reporters can't seem to avoid.

On the other hand, the gamble can pay off and there are some fine books available by journalists. Tom entered the game with determination and one great advantage.

Tom is a curious man. You are allowed to read that sentence twice because it holds two different meanings.

In the first sense, Tom is interested in everything. A phone conversation with a local alderman, a loud sneeze, household chores, fast cars, murder trials and cats hold the same fascination for him. His sense of childlike wonder allows him to view everyday as the amazing. His sources are everywhere and his ideas result from spur-of-the-moment contacts with both small and unfathomable forces – human and otherwise.

In the second sense, Tom is an unusual personality. He knows that a writer's first job is to live life and doesn't allow his profession to subvert his character. He doesn't write to his readers so much as he talks to them – sharing his world and letting them glimpse the mind of a truly unique person.

I suppose part of his approach stems from his days as a Methodist preacher in southern Arkansas. I didn't know Tom when he was a preacher, but it is my guess that his writing is simply an extension of his calling. His style is not to dictate to his readers, but to let them discover the great truths through parables of everyday life. He doesn't fall back on gummy prose. He is not cynical or smugly satirical. Tom enjoys people, and he understands them. He doesn't aim to please other writers, but reaches for the "you and me" in everybody.

When Tom first suggested *"Haley's Comments"* as the title of his column on the *Courier's* editorial page I wasn't sure what to make of it. Did he mean that he only planned to turn in a column every seventy-five years?

I needn't have worried. Tom has a preacher's tolerance for coffee and when he was on a roll managed to turn in two columns at a time (no small feat for someone working on a paper that requires you to be a reporter at city council meetings, a feature writer on the man with a squash that looks like Richard Nixon and a photographer at every "newsworthy" event in town).

But enough of this prelude stuff. When you begin reading, you'll see for yourself that Tom Haley is not just another cricket in the chorus.

Now, here are some pre-flight instructions to help you make the most of this experience. Put some flip-flops on your feet (in season), unplug the phone, trash the junk mail, hide the bills and grab a crisp apple or a firm tomato (in season). Then head for the nearest front porch, find a treehouse or head for the hammock. Find some place where you can shake off the cobwebs. Open to page 1. Enjoy.

Paul Sawyer
News Editor, The Benton Courier
1990

To The Reader

When Tom Haley walked into *The Benton Courier* newsroom in 1988, he was looking for a job. While he admitted to a lack of any newspaper experience, he possessed a genuine interest in the written word and an eagerness to hone his skills.

Up to that time, his working years had been spent as a man of the cloth. He was ready for a change of pace, he said during the job interview. He had seen a help-wanted ad for a reporter shortly after moving to Benton.

While his resume was impressive and he had been published, I wasn't certain he knew what he was getting into. A job with a community newspaper is a myriad of challenges, deadlines, stress, learning, depressions and joys. But Tom faced them all with aplomb as a fledgling reporter.

He carried a heavy workload and was in a training situation for awhile, but almost immediately asked if he could write a personal column for the editorial page. Perhaps on a weekly basis, he suggested.

Of course, he could, I said. But it would be subject to editing and rewrite. Of course, he said.

The name *"Haley's Comments"* was a natural. So are his columns. Readers comments were positive from the start. "Think about it," he writes each week. Readers do, and they like what they think about it.

He describes the taste of the best cheeseburger in Benton and readers call begging for the name of the restaurant. He refers to his wife Amanda and readers feel like she's a long-time friend. (As a matter of fact, she is a friend to many readers. She has lived in Saline County, Ark., all her life.)

"Haley's Comments" has taken off like the comet itself. He writes about his parents, his young children, his in-laws, his stepson, his childhood friends and experiences, community incidents that draw his attention, calories, exercise and frustrations in general.

He manages to link philosophy with humor, but his columns sometimes bring a tear to the eye, too, when they harbor a sentimental bent.

Topics for *"Haley's Comments"* are no problem for Tom Haley. His source is endless. He writes about life and the way it is lived, from the minor incident to the more serious of life's problems. Then he gives his readers the best of all advice as he concludes each column with "Think about it."

"Haley's Comments" appeals to all ages and the impact and interest of his columns are timeless.

Tom Haley enjoys life. In his column, he captures his joys and sorrows, his frustrations and his questions and answers and conveys those feelings to his audience on a weekly basis.

When Haley comments on life, he does a top-notch job of it.

Judy Smith
Managing Editor, The Benton Courier
July 1991

Preface

At first, *Haley's Comments* was a way to hammer out the dents in my armor. I began by scratching my pen across many memories and a host of future thoughts.

After the experience of a divorce and leaving the parish ministry, I began a new career as a columnist, staff writer and reporter for *The Benton Courier* shortly after I moved to Benton.

As the weeks mounted, readers began sharing their thoughts about some of my columns through letters and telephone calls. "People are really reading this," I thought. Some said they have clipped and saved all the columns.

One reason I chose to publish this book was the encouragement I received from the readers. The readers know me. I have shared a large part of my life with them.

My immediate family and my extended family have not escaped from making an appearance in *Haley's Comments*.

It is my wish that you find laughter and hope as you read these comments from one who only points out the common threads of life.

Tom Haley

Acknowledgments

I would like to extend my sincere appreciation to some special people for their help in the completion of this book.

To my wife, Amanda, who painstakingly edited and re-edited column after column.

To Paul Sawyer, former *Courier* news editor, for editing the columns as they first appeared in publication.

To Judy Smith, *Courier* managing editor, for allowing me to express myself in my column.

To Philip A. Felton, *Courier* staff photographer, for snapping the photograph that appears on the back page.

To Rebecca Hodges Winburn, *Courier* associate publisher, for her support and excitement of my dream.

To Dan Coston of Fayetteville, a good friend and artist, who designed the front and back cover.

To my parents, Kenneth and Phyllis Haley, for their love and support through many rough places and for their help on this "faith" journey.

To my favorite mama-in-law and daddy-in-law, Betty Jo and James "Cap" Adams, who accepted me into their family and who have provided many humorous adventures that eventually ended up on the printed page.

To all the *Courier* family, for taking time to listen while I shared my dream, and giving me encouragement and a few promises to buy this book.

And last but not least, to the *Courier* readers who took time and contacted me by cards, letters, telephone calls, and in person, telling me how much they enjoy my column. This book would not have become a reality without you.

I hope these observations of life will make you laugh a little, smile a lot, and relax on occasion.

TMH

Life with Children

*I believe the key to a happy life centers on whether
we can observe life and its wonder through the
eyes of a child.*

Meaning of Life Found at Park

On sunny days, playgrounds are usually filled to capacity. There are always sounds of children laughing as they romp among a maze of wooden structures, while others glide on swings made to resemble horses.

Rows of cars and trucks occupy parking spaces around the park's perimeter. Parents peer from these vehicles to keep tabs on their precious bundles of joy (at least that's how it appears.)

On a recent trip to Texarkana to see grandparents Kenneth and Phyllis Haley, Amanda, Jessica, John and I visited Springlake Park. There we could feed the ducks with stale bread and the kids could play until their tongues hung out.

I watched as my children blended in with the other munchkins. At 8 years of age, John didn't need Dad to watch his every move, however, it was required for 3-year-old Jessica.

A pole stood just in arm's reach from a wooden platform so children could slide down in fireman's fashion. After watching John slide down, Jessica (who thinks she can do anything her brother can) had to jump off, too. After she made a couple of trips down the pole, other small children began gathering at the launching pad for me to carefully guide them down to safety.

Two little girls – sisters – caught my attention and stole my heart. Their stringy hair needed shampooing and baths were certainly in order. Their soiled, hand-me-down clothes hung from their little frames, many sizes too large.

I observed my children and the others dressed in nicer attire and up-to-date fashions. I felt a sense of sadness swell up within me. These little girls stuck out like sore thumbs.

Even through the old clothes and the dirt, smiles of appreciation beamed from their faces. If the sisters were aware of the other children's station in life, it didn't seem to bother them. They were starved for attention. They needed to be treated as equals and made to feel special as individuals, if only for a brief moment in time. That was all that was necessary for them on that Sunday afternoon.

We aquire a lot of knowledge simply by swinging in a park swing and sliding down poles.

We enter life as squeaky-clean, antiseptic babies. Through the years, we learn to slosh through the mud, dirt and grime of life until we barely recognize ourselves in the mirror.

Even as unacceptable as we may feel or look to the world, we all need two gifts from life: to be treated as equals and to be special to at least one person.

After an hour of guiding children down poles, Amanda dubbed me the patron Saint of the Springlake Park playground. This position is really very enjoyable. You would be surprised at what a smile does for tired arms.

Walk among the children the next time you are at a park. The job of patron Saint is open to anyone. Love is the only requirement.

In his song, *The Heart of the Matter*, Grammy Award winner Don Henley asks us, "How can love survive in such a graceless age?"

We can all make a difference in this love-starved world, simply with a smile and an extended hand.

There's Life After Being Stung

It's next to impossible to venture through life without being stung, either from a business deal or an insect attack.

One Saturday morning, Amanda served the kids a delicious and special breakfast of pumpkin pancakes. (We didn't tell them what was so special about them until they gobbled down several helpings.)

Afterwards, the kids raced to the backyard to play. We sat down for a quiet and leisurely breakfast. (Pumpkin pancakes are really good. Honest.)

We heard the kids screaming, but thought nothing of the noise since this is a normal volume level while they are playing. A few moments later, the back door flew open and John ran into the kitchen. Between crying and screaming, he asked, "Am I going to die? Will I ever walk again?" Little Jessica, through her tears, wondered about her own fate.

John was more panicked than anything. I placed my hands on his chin and said, "Be quiet. You're going to live."

The kids, along with our niece, Jessica Adams, had somehow managed to excite a nest of yellow jackets.

Further investigation revealed John had about seven stings: two on the foot, two on the face, one on the eyebrow and two on the arm.

Our two-year-old, Jessica, had about 10 yellow jackets still clinging to her sweatshirt. As Amanda took her outside to brush them off, two of those little boogers flew out from under her top. Her sting count was two on the face. While she was being treated, another flew out of her training pants and stung her on her belly.

Jessica Adams was relatively lucky. She had only one sting. However, one is enough.

The two heavily-stung kids began to resemble prize fighters who had boxed 15 rounds with Mike Tyson.

After the wounded had been treated by two extremely hungry adults, life was a bit more quiet and relaxed.

Then the war stories began.

"It's a little known fact that you can't reach the age of 12 until you are stung by a wasp, yellow jacket or bee," I told the victims of the backyard war.

I related to them the time Franz Baskett and I had become victims of a similar street gang of yellow jackets while growing up in Texarkana.

Amanda recalled a childhood experience when she and Tim Elrod crawled underneath a house. During the expedition, the two explorers were suddenly face to face with a nest of those armed flying insects.

"Gasbus, look that 'em waspus," Tim had whispered. The two playmates had to keep their laughter inside until they backed out to safety. To this day, Amanda has no earthly idea what Tim's cryptic words meant.

The combination of ointment and war stories apparently calmed down the war worn soldiers.

"I'll never go out in the backyard again," John announced. By that afternoon, however, all three were running and rolling in the backyard once more.

We are all going to get stung at least once in our lifetime. Events and situations beyond our control will whirl out of nowhere and those "little stingers" are going to have our number. Count on it.

We announce to ourselves and to the world, "I'll never go out in the backyard again."

I've got war stories for every kind of sting imaginable. The sting of rejection, hopelessness, prejudice and misunderstanding are only a few from my dusty archives. Such stings soon fade away with only the memory to remind us of the pain.

Mixed Messages Are Confusing

A variety of messages are transmitted by sight and sound on our road to adulthood. Sometimes, what we learn as a child bears little resemblance to lessons learned later in life.

The confusion starts in the cradle. After a hearty bottle of milk or formula, parents begin to pound the back of their tiny bundle of joy until a beautiful sound is heard throughout the house . . . the burp.

The proud parents applaud the infant for a job well done. (As if this is the first time a little person ever did this.) "Boy, that was a big burp," a beaming mom or dad says.

About six years later, that same child opens his mouth and "burps" his full Christian name at the dinner table. No one comments on the size of that burp. Automatically, he is sent to his room until he decides to incorporate better table manners. Mixed messages are given. The child's undeveloped brain recalls a few of those backslapping incidents and the round of applause received. He becomes confused.

On the other end of the spectrum, an infant expels gas reminiscent of a trumpet blast and the whole family, including grandparents, are elated with this astonishing feat.

Years later the same noise is blamed on the dog, the cat and invisible creatures. Once again, the youngster is quarantined to his room until he decides to control his actions. Surrounded by silence, he recalls earlier childhood memories of a similar incident that produced the sound of laughter that bounced off the walls. Now he finds himself in solitary confinement. More mixed messages and confusion.

We teach children many lessons with hopes of preparing them for the real world. However, these lessons are subject to change as kids experience life for themselves. Eventually life calls them to re-learn what they have been taught.

The following is a list of a few little "phrases to live by" that I remember overhearing, or learning from experience, as a child.

* Never say anything bad about someone. If you can't say anything good, don't say anything at all. (You will be liked by all, but you could develop ulcers from being dishonest).

* Never get angry. (At least don't let anyone know your true feelings).

* Never cry if you are a boy. If you must, cry when you are alone. (This action will encourage you to believe that being human is not good enough).

* Always play by the rules. Some rules can be broken. You can bend them a little and still give the

appearance of complying with them. (This belief will help you win friends or play alone).

* Always tell the truth. You do not have to lie, just don't tell everything you know. (You will never get into trouble by telling the truth. Right?)

* Never question adults. They always have the correct answer. (When a child never questions, you will have an adult who never questions. Some questions need to be asked).

* Never take a shortcut on anything. The long way around is always best. (Some people often feel guilty by accomplishing the same task by a shorter method. Short cuts usually mean one is lazy).

* Never toot your own horn. People will think you are bragging. (You will never be allowed to feel good about what you have accomplished).

* Always go to church. All the good people attend and the bad ones stay away. (I don't think so. Some folks stay away from church because they have been hurt by the good people).

* Always report everything you find. Turn in money found on a department store floor. (Finders keepers unless you can't handle the guilt of being lucky).

* Always be right. You will always have the upper hand on someone. (This attitude will alienate you from many people).

* Never argue. It is simply not polite. (Arguing is verbally expressing angry feelings. Sometimes it's necessary).

Some folks never question situations. They follow blindly and wonder why things happen the way that they do. Perhaps we all need to re-learn a few lessons.

Little Girl Blasts Triple in Game

Playing baseball with kids in the backyard can be an enlightening experience. Neighborhood munchkins gathered as Amanda, with "whiffle" ball and bat in hand, marked the bases with my weight plates. The baseball diamond was complete and the players were anxious to begin.

Playing baseball, or any other game with kids, can be fun. Amanda and I felt the aches and pains later, but enjoyed the fun at the time. Some parents act older than they really are. You would not find them in the back yard playing baseball with a bunch of wild Commanches.

Amanda recalled with fondness the moments when her father would play pitch with her. She said this was a special time for her. Some folks would consider her to be a tomboy.

Three-year-old Jessica Haley hit a triple her first time at bat. Honest!

By the next time she was up to bat, several more neighborhood boys had arrived. "She may be 3 and a girl, but she sure can hit a baseball," John Haley said. This statement came from a 9-year-old boy who was proud of his sister.

Like Amanda, Jessica is a tomboy. I mean this in the

best sense of the word. She believes there is nothing she cannot do – she just does it. She didn't think about being a girl while she was at bat, only that she enjoyed playing baseball with the rest of the children.

I mentioned the ball game to Aunt Lois. She told me that her daughter, Sue, was a tomboy. She related one particular incident. As a Boy Scout leader, my uncle took his troop to the family's 40 acres to shoot skeet. Sue tagged along.

Girls were not supposed to enjoy shooting, but no one told Sue. She wanted to shoot some skeet. Her father allowed her to do so. "Just do your best," her father whispered into her ear. She shot much better than most of the boys, her mother said. Perhaps the next time I see her I'll christen her Annie Oakley.

Later in the backyard baseball game, we had a seventh inning stretch complete with popsicles. Then the game resumed.

During the rest of the game, I noticed Jessica's eyes getting a little sleepy. She would wander off and sit down. While I played second base, she walked over and held my hand.

The game ended about 7 o'clock that night.

Jessica played so hard that when it was time for bed, there wasn't a sign of protest.

There is always one house in the neighborhood

where kids will congregate. It seems that when John and Jessica are spending the weekend with us, kids gather.

Jessica believes she can do anything she wants to do. She is truly a free spirit. I hope her wings are never clipped as she dreams life's dreams. Jessica has a good teacher in Amanda.

Maybe the world needs to play baseball in the backyard with a few children. Perhaps, then more grownups can be free to face grownup problems with unclipped wings.

Sidewalk Chalk Artist

A kid with a piece of chalk, artistic ability, a creative mind and a driveway can be dangerous. But then, sometimes a wonderful experience can happen. This is what occurred during a recent visit by my son, John, and his sister, Jessica.

It was a slow, Saturday afternoon and not much stirring. Jessica had found some girls about her same age playing next door. John wanted to play with them but Amanda and I had said this was Jessica's time. He usually has the neighborhood boys to play with which leaves Jessica out.

Amanda was repairing a window and I was sitting on the front porch. John was perched on the steps alongside me mumbling something about there being nothing to do.

A parental thought came to mind. I said, "John, why don't you draw on the sidewalk with some sidewalk chalk." Yeah, it surprised me, too.

John has the artistic ability of drawing any one of the four Teenage Mutant Ninja Turtles. He prefers Michelangelo.

He ran quickly into the house in search of a box of colored chalk, but found only one yellow piece. John began drawing Teenage Mutant Ninja Turtles on his concrete canvas which stretched from the sidewalk that leads to the front door and then along the front of the house.

Another bright idea sputtered from my mouth. "Why don't you draw a giant Teenage Mutant Ninja Turtle on the driveway. I'll look for the box of chalk." I was on a roll.

With chalk in hand, the budding Michelangelo (not to be confused with the Teenage Mutant Ninja Turtle of the same name) began his work.

Each line was drawn with a concentrated and calculated effort. I was amazed as to how well he did in such a large area. There was a time when he could only produce small figures on an entire sheet of paper.

One at a time, the neighborhood boys began to drift by. Soon the young artist had an audience. Even one of the girls next door stopped what she was doing and watched as he carefully made several strokes with his chalk.

One can tell when an artist is proud of his work. A sparkle of accomplishment dances in the eyes.

A couple of boys asked permission to draw on his homemade canvas. One promising artist drew a cartoon of Bart Simpson.

John's ability to draw comes naturally. My father is an artist and I got my talent from him.

The walls of my parents' home were once the canvas for my mural of sorts. Inspiration struck and I transformed the light green, wooden walls into something of beauty – at least I thought so.

As I recall, I do not think my parents were as excited as I was.

I believe all of us have a need to express ourselves whether through painting, sculpture, writing or speaking. Inspiration can come at any moment. When it strikes, it is time to express ourselves.

One emotion we all need to capture is passion. We can have passion in the way we love, the way we live, the way we work, the way we write or paint. But whatever we do, we should do it with style and passion.

Child Inspires High Ambition

On a trip to Texarkana, my son, John, and I visited his MeeMaw and Pop Pop (better known as Kenneth and Phyllis Haley). Life is never dull when we are together.

The day was Sunday. We put our suits on and went to my home church, First United Methodist. John always likes to sit in the balcony. This was my favorite hangout as a youngster.

The church was pleasantly crowded, even in the balcony. The only place for us was the very first row overlooking the rest of the sanctuary. Sitting here gives you the feeling that you are about to fall over the edge.

I was proud to be standing there with my son, sharing a hymnal and singing familiar hymns.

Now bear in mind that we are standing behind the railing, looking down on the people below us. A chill ran down my spine as I thought, "What would happen if John accidently drops the hymnal on that bald-headed man?" Well, it would wake some people up. Lord knows there are some who need it, but by the Spirit, not by a Methodist hymnal.

I turned, smiled at him and gripped the book like a snapping turtle with no intentions of letting go until I heard

the last chord on the organ and we were safely seated back
into our pew.

Being with him that Sunday morning brought back
memories of a time when I was his age sitting in church.
Now, my son is just like me.

I promised him that after lunch we would go to the
old Arkansas High School football field and play some
football.

As I walked onto the field, I could hear the band
playing our fight song, "Dixie." I could see the crowd
yelling and cheering. I could feel the excitement within me as
I was about to run through the goalposts as a defensive
tackle for the Arkansas High Razorbacks, hoping I wouldn't
trip over my feet and feel really embarrassed.

A brisk breeze brought me back to 1988 along with
shouts of, "Throw the ball, Dad. Come on, throw the ball!"

I looked around to where wooden bleachers once
stood and saw grass growing where the track had been. I
saw a 7-year-old boy running where his father ran about 20
years ago.

We had fun together on that beautiful November
afternoon. As a father, I just looked at my son and wondered
what he was going to do with his life, what career he would
choose and what influence I would have on him.

We can show our children where we've walked, but
they must take their own steps into the future. We can talk

about our lessons from the past, but they must live out their future and learn from their own experiences.

No matter what career John chooses, no matter what he does in his life and no matter how he lives out his life, I want him to know one important truth – I will always love him.

He seems to ask those questions. You know the questions. One evening a couple of years ago at the dinner table, John and I had just finished singing a Paul Simon song, when he looked up at me and asked, "Dad, what are you going to be when you grow up?"

He caught me off guard and I didn't have an answer. I've had time to think about it. I've been through many winding turns and bumpy roads since then, but I do have an answer for him now. I'm going to be happy.

That's what I'm going to be . . . now! How about you? How long has it been since you were happy and laughed for no apparent reason? Well, that's too long.

Hanging Ten on a Skateboard

Ocean waves are not the only waves that come from California. Waves of trends and fads seem to flow eastward, making their way through Arkansas.

In past years, what started on the west coast would ultimately show up several years later in the "Natural" state. However, with the advent of satellite programming, years are not necessary. Influences, via a telvision set, can be projected overnight.

While guys are "hanging ten" on surfboards off Malibu Beach, Arkansans are riding concrete waves on skateboards. As a child, I would ride skateboards down County Avenue in Texarkana.

Skateboards were not the sleek and awesome devices we see today. A short, flat board with roller skate wheels, separated and nailed to the bottom at each end was the "Arkansas skateboard."

I tried my hand, or better yet, my feet at skateboarding, but after several spills, I decided to give up on the thought of ever mastering that feat.

Amanda apparently rode the concrete waves better than me. She told me that as a young teen, she bought a skateboard from The Bryant Pharmacy that cost less than

$20.

Times have changed.

Today, skateboarding has returned in full force with a variety of changes. It has evolved into a technological wonder and requires state of the art equipment. Every dimension must be accurate. The wheels are balanced and larger. The board is wider with a curved stern. Prices vary for these concrete jets, but for about $80, a good board can be yours.

Amanda and I choose to stay on our feet now. We have our usual walking route set up around our neighborhood. On one trek, we noticed a young man performing some flips and riding rather decently on his board. He was fast becoming a "wizard on wheels."

Ty Blacklock has gotten the art of skateboarding down, but it doesn't come easy to him or any other person. He said he tries to learn at least a couple of tricks a day. It's more than I could do. My trick would be just to stay on.

I guess I have always been fascinated by wheels. In the beginning, I would ride my father's high chair. It was one of those that sported iron wheels. Since that time, my father-in-law and I have refurbished it. This antique is in my dinning room now.

As a kid, I went through my "building a sports car" phase. With several boards, four wheels, nuts and bolts, and some rope, I fashioned my racer.

My race track was the sidewalk beside my home. There was a slight slant to it, so heavy pushing was not required too often. The brakes needed a bit of work. Driving this wild machine took someone with a little experience in the art of rope steering.

I believe imagination played a large part in early sports car construction. What I envisioned about the car became true for me.

Imagination can be a key to our living happy and contented lives. Grown-ups seem to have lost the power of this quality. Visualize what you want to be, how you want to act, and where you want your life to take you; then proceed with both oars in the water.

Using our imagination in this way could be the start of a new you and me. It sure beats the heck out of envisioning a person being controlled by life rather than directing his or her destiny.

Ty, keep seeing yourself conquering the concrete waves and you will do it. As for the rest of us, we will all have our own waves to conquer.

Imagine a smooth ride.

Reading Fires the Imagination

Read any good books lately?

These hot temperatures remind me of those summer vacation days gone by when I would make my way to the Texarkana Public Library.

The library was a kingdom ready to be conquered. I remember being greeted by the wonderful feeling of anticipation as I opened the huge, wooden library doors. The aroma of adventure loomed in the air. Shelf after shelf bulged with books. The library served as a door opening into magical places and my library card was the key to get there. Tightly grasped in my hand, it allowed me to become a time traveler.

Reading allows you to go to far off places without leaving your chair. In all my travels and adventures, only reading could project me back into the past and forward into the future

I played baseball with the greats, Babe Ruth and Mickey Mantle. I engaged in battles alongside Robin Hood and his Merry Men.

Most of all, I love biographies. It is fascinating to read about the struggles, the joys and the victories in the lives of other people.

My wife, Amanda, likes to read. As a junior high student, she read every book in the school library. "It was a small library at that time," she said.

I personally believe it should be listed in the book of literary feats, no matter how small the library.

The beeps of the video game "Super Mario Brothers" cannot match the sound of metal swords clashing and the smell of smoking fire-arrows that rise off the printed page as the story of a raging battle is read.

The difference between video games and books is nestled in the fact that books fire up your imagination. Video games limit your perception. Really, it is only what you see is what you get; nothing more, nothing less.

I like to play an occasional video game, but not too often. I'm a novice at the game. My son can beat me. He's a video wizard.

Our fast-paced lifestyle limits our concentration. We make little time for ourselves to read long articles. It seems there is only time to glance through the newspaper and catch glimpses of blurred headlines. The story is read only if the headline is catchy enough for our tastes.

I must confess something. In school, I used Cliff Notes along with the Classic Illustrated comic book for some book reports. They were a part of my personal library and served as resource material for my homework when I was behind in my reading.

If any of my former teachers are reading this, forgive me. I've changed.

Have you read any good books lately? You should. You need a vacation.

The Most Important Circus Job

A day at the circus is like no other day. It is truly "the greatest show on earth."

Amanda and I went to Little Rock to the Ringling Bros. and Barnum & Bailey Circus. We weren't alone. Traveling with us were John, Jessica and our niece, Jessica Adams.

I had seen smaller versions of circuses, but never the "big" one. We saw clowns, clowns and more clowns who made us forget about our troubles and offered us smiles. We held our breath and said silent prayers for the safety of the tightrope walkers, the two crazy, but well-paid men who were shot from a gigantic cannon and the trapeze families flying through the air.

Three rings of amazing, simultaneous performances were almost too much to take in. "Did you see that bear walking on his paws?" "Yeah, but did you see that dancing baboon?" No, but did you see those elephants sitting up on their back legs?"

We also had three rings of excitement in the stands. Our kids, all under nine years of age, were a handful to watch.

In every circus, one act receives top billing. This

year it was *Tahar: The Moroccan Master*. This alligator tamer
was indeed impressive.

As the parade of acts entered and were announced,
Tahar rode in on an elephant surrounded by African
tribesmen dancing, singing and sounding like some of the
"rap" music currently on the Top 40 record charts.

After taking the alligators from cages, he would
hypnotize them by moving his hands and staring them
down. Tahar forgot about one 'gator who crawled over the
ring wall and ventured near the people in the front row. I
could see the spectators hadn't forgotten because they
couldn't take their eyes off that green mouth full of teeth.
Tahar rushed over and hypnotized him. The alligator never
moved a muscle – until the end of the act.

When the alligator awoke from his trance, he once
again moved toward the front row with his mouth wide
open. People began to jump up into their seats. After Tahar
retrieved the 'gator, one mother was seen carrying her little
boy away, perhaps to the restroom.

Performers dream of becoming the top act. The
endless years of practice are rewarded as their talents are
showcased under the Big Top.

The circus employs hundreds of workers. Everyone
has a special job to do. However, we never read about the
jobs of some circus workers. Their responsibilities are not
glamorous. They wear uniforms, not costumes. Yet their job

is vitally important in the smooth running of the show.

With shovel in hand, these workers keep a sharp eye out for elephants, horses, and zebras leaving big surprises on the floor. This accomplishment is not something you would write home about.

Children rarely miss anything. Almost in unison every child in the audience shouted, "Did you see what that elephant did?"

Try saying, "Hold it, hold it, hold it!" or "Stop it, stop it, stop it!" to a three-ton pachyderm that's not housebroken.

Between spilled snowcones and the breathtaking circus acts, Amanda and I were on the edge of our seats for two and a half hours.

The clowns made us laugh and the alligators made us squirm. The men with the pooper scoopers, well, they made us appreciate our own jobs.

Every person's job is important. It's all in how you look at it. Would you rather wrestle an alligator or a shovel?

Some Fears Live In Us

All of us have a certain amount of fears. We often wonder where they originated, why these feelings continue and how long they will remain?

Fear – *n.* 1. A feeling of anxiety and agitation caused by the presence or nearness of danger; evil or pain – according to Mr. Webster.

Some folks have phobias (irrational or excessive fears) about being closed up in tight spaces, flying in an airplane, failure and success and my favorite – snakes.

My late Uncle Harold played a trick on me that included a snake. He knew how squeamish I was of the slithering creatures in my younger days. A large snake met its fate at his hands one afternoon. He carefully coiled it up and strategically placed the reptile on the steps leading to his front door.

The phone rang at my house. It was my uncle inviting me over for something. As I walked the short three blocks to his house, I tried to figure out why he had called.

Uncle Harold knew that most of the time my head was in the clouds. My mind was definitely out of the clouds when I noticed this gigantic snake coiled up on the steps and ready to strike (or so I thought).

He told me later (he was laughing too hard at the time to speak) that I must have jumped five feet backwards from the snake. I assume his point was that I needed to be more aware of things around me. I was nothing BUT aware from that moment on, especially each time I traveled to his house.

Asking ourselves some specific questions might alleviate some fears.

* "What's the worst that could happen?" In this case the thought of dying ran through my mind. After I made my record-breaking, reverse long jump, my feet turned to concrete blocks making further escape impossible.

* "Is this fear real or imaginary?" It is as real as rain. I can't stand snakes. I would rather fight a bear with no weapon than tangle with a slithering reptile. There may be a chance with a bear. I could always run. With a snake, I freeze in my steps. I have been told all my life that a snake is as afraid of you as you are of it. Oh, yeah! Right!

* "What's the root of the fear?" I'll tell you the root of my fear. It is fear of the unknown. Snakes cannot be trusted. You don't know what they'll do, where they will go or how fast they will travel to get to you.

Even as I write this, the fear of snakes still exists in me. While watching the movie Indiana Jones and the Raiders of the Lost Ark, I screamed out loud when Jones fell into a pit of coiling, slithering and wiggling snakes. Let me wrestle a bear any day.

Most of us become very religious and pray during times of fear. These prayers are rather short and sweet – "God. Help me!" Somehow, we usually manage to muster up enough courage to face a particular situation. I recall this little quote someone once said, "Courage is fear that has said its prayers." It works for me.

Fear could originate from losing something like a job, a home, loved ones or even our health. We came into this world with nothing and we'll leave this world with nothing. I haven't seen any U-Haul trailers hooked up behind a funeral hearse lately. Have you?

Perhaps President Franklin D. Roosevelt was right when he said, "Let me assert my firm belief that the only thing we have to fear is fear itself."

Columnist Tickled by Kids

Just when you think kids only play video games for hours on end, they fool you. I had a very pleasant experience recently, talking with the fifth-grade class at Ringold Elementary School in Benton. Actually, they made my day. I floated out of the school's cafeteria on Cloud 9 after I left the speaking engagement.

I was there because of the Partners in Education Program between the school and *The Courier*. In the introduction, the principal asked the large group how many read my column. I was surprised to see about three fourths of their hands raised. Can you imagine how excited I felt? These were fifth-grade students.

I told them briefly about how I became a staff writer, reporter and columnist at the newspaper. Then I opened the floor for questions. I had no idea of the variety of questions they would ask. I quickly found out. The kids did not hold back.

They liked my red, high-top sneakers. I told them the red shoes were my lucky shoes. Recalling one of my favorite stories, *The Wizard of Oz*, I mentioned Dorothy's ruby red slippers and how she clicked her heels together and said, "There's no place like home."

"When I'm having a bad day, I just click my heels together and say, 'tomorrow's another day'," I told the kids.

They asked questions about particular columns. One boy asked about the "chicken-fried steak" column and how it came to be.

Others asked where I get my ideas and do I have a favorite column.

Some questions were meatier than others, such as; did I ever fail a subject in school, receive a paddling, or get kicked out of school. I answered "yes" to all of the above.

I told them the reason I attended school was because all my friends were there. My least favorite subject was English.

"Life has a way of surprising us," I said. "Who would have thought I would one day earn a living writing words?"

The kids wanted to know if I had any plans to write a column about them. I said yes.

I asked them what they wanted me to say about them. The consensus was to write that they were well-mannered and smart. One student said," Say we were cool!"

The children were kind and courteous in spite of the afternoon session and thoughts of summer vacation only a week away.

After my time ended, I received the ultimate compliment. I was asked for my autograph by many of the kids. I was tickled.

Sometimes, when we least expect it, kids often fool us. Just ask any elementary school teacher. They have stories to tell.

It's Baseball, Not 'Boot Camp'

Remember how relaxing it once was to sit in the bleachers and watch kids play a baseball game? Those days are gone in some towns.

Remember shouting words of encouragement to your children when they dropped a fly ball or struck out? The yelling is still in the air, but the words are not always words of support. We are a people who believe our kids must be No. 1 in everything.

Our sons and daughters must be the fastest runners, the homerun hitters and be able to catch a long fly ball with their teeth. If they can't do any of these, well, they are not really trying and may even be an embarrassment to their parents. The attitude of a parent who is obsessed with the idea that his child has got to be the absolute best, tells more about the parent than it does about the child.

What about sports-minded parents?

The ones who coach from the bleachers and always seem to know exactly what to do, are seldom the ones who give support to their kids with many hours of coaching the team or providing backyard practice.

The parents who yell profanities at the umpires ought to be penalized. The umps are doing the best job they can do. Maybe those parents should be forced to umpire games for two weeks. They may change their attitude once the "umping" shoe is on the other foot.

The parents who make unkind and hurting remarks to the kids from the other teams obviously have vinegar running through their veins.

What about the coaches?

They are so determined to win that nothing less than the best players get to walk onto the field. The coaches put so much pressure on the kids and criticize them so much that some never want to play ball again.

Some coaches seem to think playing games through the night is healthy for their young players and their parents. I heard recently of a 6 year old baseball player who had just found out which end of the bat to use. This youngster dragged home about 1 a.m. after a game.

Let's let our children be children. They grow up too quickly. Some children are forced to be "little adults" and never get a chance to enjoy being a kid.

Some adults have never grown up and don't know the meaning of responsibility.

Then there are people like you and me. We believe it is time to allow our kids to play ball and have fun. Let the kids enjoy the game without the added burden of perfection. Have we lost sight of the main reason kids are playing in the first place? Why do coaches and parents play for blood?

Relax. It's only a game.

It is time to return to those days when attending a baseball game was fun for the parents and playing in a game was fun for the kids.

Life at Holidays

Most of us are nervous wrecks during each holiday season. We are anxious for their arrival and elated at their departure. Holidays are liked well-planned weddings. No matter what tragedies occur during the service, the couple always ends up married.

Amnesia on Thanksgiving Day

On Thanksgiving Day, the aroma of turkey and dressing, cranberry sauce and homemade rolls dance around our nostrils. Impatient cries asking, "when will we eat" circulate around the room. A variety of cooks will attempt to soothe the famished beasts with a nibble or two from the sacred bird.

As the table is set and napkins are carefully placed in our laps, we announce to each member of our families just how grateful we are and offer our thankful prayers.

It is tradition.

I believe it is very difficult to be thankful:

* If we have never had to go through lean years worrying about how we are going to stretch the few coins jingling in our pockets to feed our families.

* If we have had to go without food while others stuff their faces.

* If we have never had to fight for adequate housing where the roof didn't leak, cold wind didn't blow through the cracks and each child had a bed of his own.

* If we have never experienced the loss of our jobs, our identity, and had to rely on the graciousness of others.

* If we have never reluctantly had to say to our

children that we simply can't afford new school clothes because what little money we do have, must go to pay the utility bills.

* If we have never suffered the agony of losing everything we own in the angry winds of a tornado, the shaking of an earthquake, the flames of a house fire or the raging waters of a flood.

* If we have never faced rejection of employment because we were handicapped, poor, didn't have a college degree or were members of a minority.

* If we have never lacked medical attention because we couldn't afford quarterly insurance premiums.

* If we have never had to be without that special someone in our lives who gave us support.

* If we have never known the freedoms associated with living in a country where prison is not an alternative to speaking our convictions.

* If we have never been without the security of some form of reliable transportation.

* If we have never had to deal with physical handicaps which impair the ability to read inspiring novels, see beautiful sunsets or hear the birds warble spring songs.

Thanksgiving can be a time of giving thanks even if we haven't experienced these tragedies. However, awareness of our many blessings can easily escape us. To "thank" we must "think." Maybe we need to cultivate thankful thoughts in order to be truly grateful.

When Christ healed the 10 lepers, we assume all were thankful, however, only one remembered what it was like to be an outcast and returned to express his gratitude.

It is never enough to simply say how thankful we are. We need to reach out to others with healing hands to demonstrate our own gratitude.

What's Your Christmas Wish?

Children learn by observing big people. They are always watching us.

Amanda and I were shopping in a variety store one Christmas and noticed the small daughter of a Christmas-shopping mother. The little girl clutched a new note pad and pencil and said, "Now I can write down all the things I want for Christmas."

My parents have asked me more than once what I want for Christmas? A Christmas "wish list" circulated through *The Benton Courier* office and I strained to write down some items.

Honestly, I find it very difficult to think of anything I want for Christmas. At the age when "visions of sugar plums danced in my head," all it took was a Sears and Roebuck Christmas catalog and plenty of time. The pages were worn out by the time December arrived. I could recite my toy list with no problem.

My list this year is made up of things that can't be purchased. For instance:

* More time to spend with my wife, Amanda. It seems life calls us to do this, go there and fix this, leaving us with too little "companion" time.

* A new back. This 1952 model has seen better days.

* A waist just a bit smaller than the one I'm carrying around with me. This could be part of my back problem.

* More hair on the top of my head. The length is long, but there is a thin patch on top that is a prime target for a sunburn.

* Fewer surprises. I don't mind the nice ones like getting a refund check in the mail. I'm talking about surprises like unexpected medical, insurance, and home repair bills.

* Time to read a few books and type on my computer. There are several books of my own that are inside me ready to leap out onto the page.

Other Christmas wishes I have are for the nation are:

* Neighborhoods, communities, cities and towns working together for the common good of all residents instead of fighting among themselves and producing nothing but deep-seated resentment.

* Elected officials representing local, state and national governments who are more interested in people than ego, prestige and self-centered political aspirations.

* A good dose of self-esteem and self-worth, gently blended with love, dreams and hopes for each person on this planet.

* An end to all wars. We've had our share of

fighting, but if called, we will go.

      * A solution to the problems of poverty, starvation and hatred.

      These are only a few of my Christmas wishes. Perhaps you have some ideas for your own list.

Christmas From the Inside Out

Have you noticed that more and more people are climbing into attics and storage buildings to pull out Christmas decorations earlier than they did last year?

I know. I know. Some "Bah Humbug" folks have already made their observations and judgments about "those" people who decorate early.

I love the season and wish the feeling could last all year long. However, there are some people who are traditional and will not decorate until the proper time – the middle of December.

I have seen some beautiful homes decorated with candle-like lights in every window, enormous trees which cover the living room corner and even Santa and his reindeer on the roof. These houses are indeed impressive.

In some parts of the city, a simple worn-out wreath hangs on a front door that desperately needs a few coats of paint. A lighted snowman hangs in a window covered with plastic to keep out the cold wind. These homes are beautiful from the inside out. Even though it is a lean year for some, the spirit of Christmas somehow manages to slip unnoticed through the crack in the front door.

At churches, schedules of Christmas events are

mailed to eager parishioners. There are potluck dinners, a Christmas pageant, a choir's Christmas cantata, Holy Communion and the ever popular Sunday School class parties.

We flip through the pages of the Good Book until we find the Christmas Story and read it for the one-hundredth time. We often dismiss the mention of the barn in this ancient tale. Barns are buildings in which we walk very carefully so we don't step in something. As we enter, our nostrils catch a pungent odor that encourages us to find the quickest way out. A barn, of all places, was the birthplace of a King.

Each Christmas we tear our hair out trying to find gifts for our family and friends. This task becomes more difficult with the passing of each Christmas. Scores of fathers are the most difficult people to purchase gifts for. It is so frustrating trying to find just the right gift.

I have never really seen my father get very excited about Christmas gifts. Bottles of Old Spice, Williams' Lectric Shave and a pair of Jiffy houseshoes made up the standard gift giving for him.

Dad's favorite color is green. The shade of green on cold, hard cash. However, he has been known to accept a check or two.

Christmas should be full of surprises.

The shepherds worshiped the Babe, the three

wisemen presented their priceless gifts of gold, frankincense and myrrh, and the heavenly host serenaded the little King with their gift of song. A dirty Bethlehem barn was transformed from the inside out. The Babe's presence continues to beautify us in the same manner.

Tell me. What do you get someone who has everything? Perhaps love.

Christmas Holds Unique Images

One mid-November afternoon, I thought I heard Christmas carols being played over the loud speaker in a department store. No, I know I heard them.

Don't get me wrong, I love Christmas music. The sounds are magical. But why do stores need to start so blooming early?

I know. It's economics. Advertise early. Move that Christmas stock. Make people think of beautifully wrapped packages artistically placed under a tree bulging with an assortment of ornaments.

Think Christmas gifts.

Christmas is the time when we promised ourselves faithfully last year that our gift buying next year would be finished by November, in order to allow us time to really enjoy the season.

Christmas is a time when lonely people are exceptionally lonely and the hungry and homeless people find there is still no room in the inn.

Christmas is a time when our emotions are at their highest. We push ourselves to the limit to do everything perfect. We try to buy the perfect gift, prepare the perfect meal, host the perfect party and enjoy the perfect Christmas.

We end up on the verge of tears and wearing our feelings on our sleeves.

As long as there are bathrobes, sticks and children, the story of why we celebrate Christmas will always be told. Do you remember a "perfect" Christmas pageant? My guess is you don't.

You may remember the little angels with crooked halos coming in late, the wisemen with beards too large for their faces who lose their way to the manger, the little fat shepherd who forgot his lines, and Mary misplacing Baby Jesus somewhere in the barn. However, we never recall a perfect pageant.

It is amazing! After all the packages are unwrapped, all the parties are finished, all the whirlwind shopping sprees have ceased, we catch our breath and say, "I wish Christmas came more than once a year. Now, I think it is time for another glass of eggnog."

Who are we kidding? Did we forget the wall to wall humanity breathing down our necks to get that sweater for half-of-half price? Did we fail to remember the late night hours of putting together bicycles and discovering one bolt was missing? What about the heated discussion over which grandparent's home to attend for Christmas dinner? What about the Christmas gift for Dad we bought in July, but we hid it so well that we couldn't find until New Year's Day? Some things we choose to forget.

Maybe this Christmas will be the Christmas we have always wanted. Gifts of friendship will be wrapped in hugs and kisses. Love will be expressed in multicolored words and actions.

After all, Jesus is the reason for the season; not department store pre-Christmas sales.

May the joy of giving, the hope of love and peace in our hearts be among our gifts this season.

The Perfect Christmas Gift

Christmas.

This emotionally charged day was once filled with the anticipation of receiving an assortment of brightly wrapped gifts. Now, it's a season engulfed in time, space, travel, and money.

First – time. Who has it? Some people have nothing but time on their hands, while others carry calendars saturated with places to go, people to see, and gifts to buy written on every page. They make a list of lists that are checked more than twice. Some people are up to their holiday necks with commitments to attend parties, family gatherings and other social functions.

Second – space. Where do we find it? 'Tis the season to be . . . hectic, cramped, hurried, pushed, and gouged. Pressure tightens an imaginary band around our hands and heads as we battle crowds in stores. Walls close in as shopping carts seem to increase in size. Every item we ordered earlier in the year is back-ordered.

Third – travel. Who wants to? Millions of yuletide travelers load up their cars with kids and presents. These nomads strike out on our nation's highways to make sure every friend and relative is visited. Sounds a bit like St.

Nick's job description to me.

Fourth – money. Where to get it? For reasons known and unknown, we buy an avalanche of gifts. We sing all the classic Christmas carols with a little twist like "Deck the Halls with Revolving Charges," "It's Beginning to Look a Lot Like Bankruptcy," "All I want for Christmas is My Two Week Vacation," and "We Wish You Would Buy Some More Christmas."

Hold it! Time Out! Do you ever get the feeling that Christmas controls you rather than you controlling Christmas? Granted, Christmas announces hope to a weary world, but not to weary shoppers.

When we were younger, Christmas meant getting out of school, noses pressed tightly against store windows and the anticipation of waking up to gifts left under the tree by a fat old elf.

Now, as adults, Christmas rolls over us like a giant snowball picking up everything in its pathway. By New Year's Day, we are just happy it's over and we've survived.

I'm not a Scrooge, nor do I possess a "Bah! Humbug!" attitude. I love this season of warmth, joy and the possibility of peace. But, I, along with others, would like to regain control of Christmas.

We become so frustrated with this whole Christmas thing because some folks forget its true meaning. Campaigns abound encouraging people to put Christ back into

Christmas. If the truth is known, Christ never left. According to a famous lecturer, Christ doesn't call us to the malls during the Christmas Season. Christmas can be a very beautiful experience for us. How we approach the season is our choice.

God wrapped the first Christmas gift in swaddling clothes and put Him into our hearts. Perhaps our gift should be to wrap ourselves in love, peace, joy and hope and give our hearts back to Him.

Feast of Laughter

According to historians, the first Thanksgiving was celebrated about the year 1621, give or take a turkey or two.

I met my new family Thanksgiving Day, 1989. It was the best one I have ever experienced. For me it truly was a time to be thankful.

As the new son-in-law, I felt warmth and acceptance from my new family at James and Betty Jo Adams' house. Laughter was passed around the table like second and third helpings of the best turkey and dressing that ever entered my mouth. Frozen cranberry salad was a new dish for me and I could have eaten it all. (I understand that last year they had to chisel it out of the bowl.)

Have you ever eaten "upside-down brocolli casserole?" The ingredients are the same as the original recipe. Mix the ingredients, place it in a casserole dish, take it out of the oven, and put it in the car. After you arrive at your destination, open your car door and let it fall out on the ground still covered. My new aunt and uncle, Orville and Eve, devised this recipe. It was delicious any way you tossed it.

Amanda and I co-authored the deviled eggs. (I mashed the hard boiled eggs yolks.) Concerning me helping, her mother said, "Oh, I forgot, YOU have help."

I rolled to the car after lunch. It was that last piece of mincemeat pie that did it. Speaking of desserts, there was a lengthy discussion about the necessity of dessert plates. Most of us, however, just cleared a place on our dinner plates for a piece or two of pie.

Amanda and I drove back to our house to do a bit of housework. Perhaps we said we would think about doing some housework.

Actually, too stuffed adults crawled into bed and began to watch the Dallas Cowboys play the Philadelphia Eagles and fell asleep until halftime. (These days, the Cowboys often lull viewers to sleep.) Thanksgiving Day is not complete without a football game, so we watched the game in spurts.

After the game, it was back to the Adams' dinner table to finish off the feast. This time, my new son, Nathan, was in the den sporting a pierced left ear and longish hair that appeared to foreshadow a long stretch between trims. Some folks say we are a lot alike. (We are. It's like a couple of humorous bookends. As soon as we get our act together we're taking it on the road.)

More laughter and more food followed through the course of yet another meal, which was just as delicious as the first. This time I was full to the brim, topped off by a piece of Mamma Betty's pecan pie. This time, I used a dessert plate, bringing a smile to Mamma's face.

I asked where the scales were located. (I needed to weigh the damage.) The digital numbers flashed like a Las Vegas slot machine on a Saturday night. The heavy truth unfolded at 230 pounds. Married life has been good to me. I've gained only 21 pounds due to heavenly bliss.

As the final bubbling of two Alka-Selzer tablets reached the top of my glass and the sun set in the west, I thanked God for my new family.

Giving ourselves as Thanksgiving gifts to each other really made the day special, one I won't soon forget. If you didn't get a chance to give yourself as a gift you still have time before Christmas.

Mother Recalls Christmas Gift

Christmas is the time we celebrate the birth of Christ. Churches go to great lengths and expense to present cantatas, Christmas pageants, church-wide potluck dinners and even a live Nativity scene.

Our attention is focused on a baby boy wrapped in swaddling clothes, lying in a cattle trough, nestled in a barn.

As the story goes, the wealthy wisemen brought priceless gifts of gold, frankincense and myrrh. Struggling shepherds left grazing sheep on a hillside to experience the wonder of the little King.

Some women, who become mothers during this time of the year, seem to identify with Mary, the mother of Jesus. Their newborn babe is as special to them as Jesus was to Mary. My wife was one of them. Hearing the ageless Christmas Story and seeing the evidence of the Christmas season all around her created a special atmosphere for this young mother. The feeling continues even as I write this column.

The people born at this time are annually squeezed in between a Christmas tree and a New Year's Day football game. They have the distinction of being born on Christmas Eve, Christmas Day or the day after Christmas.

Nathan, Amanda's son and my cosmic twin, was born on Christmas Eve. She said celebrating Nathan's birthday never really posed any problems. In the early years, she had birthday parties a couple of weeks before Christmas. Gifts were always presented in birthday paper, never Christmas wrappings.

Amanda believes Nathan was God's gift to her on that Christmas Eve in 1970, although she didn't actually get to see or hold him until he was presented to her by a nurse on Christmas Day.

"Nathan could never be compared to the Son of God, nor me to Mary," she says with a laugh.

Nathan, who celebrates his 20th birthday today, has come a long way from that little baby boy, tucked inside a red Christmas stocking fresh from St. Vincent's Hospital in Little Rock. (The stockings were made by the ladies auxiliary to hold babies born around Christmas.)

Amanda, like most mothers, can still see him cradled in that stocking. This vision continues even as Nathan matures as a man. Remembrance is one of those wonderful gifts God gives parents.

He has been taught well by the love and care of his mother. Nathan is his own person and possesses many qualities that mark him as one of a kind. Being a Christmas Eve baby hasn't caused him any hardships. He will probably laugh about it for many years to come.

As for his mother, she will cherish the day and remember the moment her eyes first met her new born baby boy.

In this season, let us remember the Bethlehem baby and the moment our eyes first met his.

A Day of Love

It is St. Valentine's Day and love is in the air. Most of us stare at rows and rows of sentimental cards on store shelves. It is an adventure just searching for the right Valentine card. This feeling is like being hungry, but not knowing what you want to eat. You open your refrigerator door and just stare.

The Hallmark Card Co. has helped us say the right words to the ones we love for years. They have a card for every occasion from Groundhog's Day to Christmas.

Receiving a heart-shaped box of Russell Stover's candy wrapped in red cellophane on Valentine's Day is a Haley family tradition.

My girlfriend in the sixth grade was Deanne Rue. She was at least a foot taller than I and her father was a Baptist preacher. I have always lived dangerously.

Valentine's Day was slowly creeping up and I needed to get her a present. I was a little short of cash, so I got a job stacking two or three cords of wood for Uncle Harold. He gave me five dollars.

I shuffled down to the drugstore for a box of candy.

In class the next day, I wrote her a note telling her I wanted to kiss her. She wrote back with instructions to meet her behind the old cafeteria building during lunch.

I couldn't wait until lunch. My stomach was growling, but not from the lack of food. It finally hit me. I had just told Deanne I wanted to kiss her.

Beads of sweat began to pop out on my forehead. My throat was getting tight. I wondered what kind of mess had I managed to step into with such awkward grace?

Sure enough, right after lunch, we met.

I believe she was more willing to kiss than I was. I was so nervous I thought my heart would beat out of my chest.

I told her to close her eyes and count to 10 and I would kiss her. The command sounded more like orders for a firing squad than exchanging lip prints.

I don't remember the "kiss."

What I do remember is the crowd of kids peering around the corner of the building. They knew this event was about to take place. She had told a few girlfriends and they had spread the word like wildfire.

I can still hear the laughter and feel the embarrassment.

Valentine's Days have come and gone. Most of them I can't recall. There are a few of us who remember our first kiss and who would like to forget it. However, most people enjoy reminiscing about a particularly memorable one.

Valentine's Day, Feb. 14, 1989, was one that I will

remember for at least seventy years.

By the time you read this, I will have been married to my sweetheart for quite some time. She is the beautiful blue collar worker and the one who has cured me of an addition to the "Boob" tube.

She is the one who encourages me in the midst of dark moments; the one who gives new meaning to the words caring, loving, and giving.

She has a heart of gold filled with goodness. She brightens up my cloudy days with her smile.

I guess I am just a hopeless romantic. Who else would get married on a Tuesday afternoon just because it is Valentine's Day?

We all need a special person in our lives.

Don't worry so much about the right card. Don't fret over all the chocolate treats saturated with loads of calories. Flowers are beautiful, but for only a brief moment. Give the gift that keeps giving over and over. Give love. One size fits all. You determine the warranty.

You can say it with flowers. You can say it with candy. You can say it with almost anything. Just say it.

I gave my Valentine a simple gold ring which says, "Amanda, I love you!"

Food For a New Year's Voyage

Once again, the dawn of a New Year eagerly awaits us whether we are ready or not. Parties, dances and other celebrations are planned.

The whole New Year's thing revolves around the passage of time. I believe time is the miracle healer.

If we have experienced either a physical or emotional hurt during the past year, as time fades away, so will those painful feelings.

However, if the past year has given us happy moments to remember, time will not erase them. They will live in our minds for many years.

We sing *Auld Lang Syne,* lift high our champagne glasses and make a toast to a fresh start or a new beginning.

Here are some thoughts I will try to remember on my journey through the new year:

* *What goes around, comes around.*

There are some sick individuals in the world that have nothing better to do than to gossip, back bite and criticize other people. These folks are sad and need pity. They are obviously unhappy with their own lives and they try to make others as miserable as they seem to be. Devious people like these, unfortunately, know exactly which button to push to make us squirm, get angry or loose our cool. For the New Year, we will not allow these scumbags to determine how we act, feel or think. As far as we are concerned, they do not exist.

* *This too shall pass.*

Our mistakes find ways of haunting us. We seem to run into their hidden reminders behind every corner. Our minds scream out, "Enough is enough!" A New Years's resolution may be to remember that time will remove these thorns in our flesh.

* *Attitude adjustment in process.*

Sometimes, we experience circumstances in life that cannot be changed. However, we do hold the power to change our attitude about them. Beginning this New Year, we can view life with more positive thoughts than negative, look at what God and life are trying to communicate to us in each situation, and remember that even though we haven't arrived yet, at least we are headed in the right direction.

* *Live in the here and now.*

Many of us live out our lives holding on to the past or daydreaming about the future. In either case, we are prevented from celebrating the "here and now." Remembering the past can be a comfort to us. However, it is not necessary to set up housekeeping there. Thinking about the possibilities of the future and planning for tomorrow can be exciting, but real living must be accomplished with our heads out of the clouds and our feet firmly planted on the ground.

  * *God has the final word.*

Many of us hesitate to believe that the Almighty has each day of our lives programmed. If that were the case, we would move a bit smoother through life and avoid all pitfalls and failures. I, myself, do not believe we are robots controlled by a "cosmic" computer operator. I do believe in and have experienced God's compassion, love and forgiveness. In the end, He has the final say. Thank God!

On our journey through this coming year, may we love more, laugh more and grow more.

Life with Animals

I am constantly amazed at the lessons of life taught by God's creatures. I wonder if we teach them anything.

Tails Chased by Dogs and Folks

Our cat, Dreyfuss, decided to seek greener pastures some time back. I guess cats do that, being independent and all. I was attached to Dreyfuss, my first cat ever, and now he was gone.

Exit Dreyfuss. Enter Thomasina – my namesake. Amanda surprised me with a cute little bundle of gray possum-like fur with a pink ribbon around its neck.

Months earlier, Amanda had brought Newly, the horse-puppy, into the kitchen draped over her shoulders. (Something she can't do now.) "Isn't he cute?" she said. "Can we keep him?" She found this feisty little puppy wandering around the Alright Printing Company on Military Road. He is a mixed breed; mixed with what we do not know. As he grows, he appears to be a mixture of St. Bernard and palomino pony.

One lazy afternoon, we peered out the window and watched as Newly not only chased his tail, but held on to it with his teeth and walked sideways. He did this about three times. Where is a video camera when you need it?

Newly would lie down and try to snatch his tail and hold on. After several tries, he managed to get up on all fours. He would parade proudly, pondering why he ever wanted to accomplish this trick. I wonder if the answer ever came to him?

Perched in the window, Thomasina watched the dog go through several body contortions. Cats have a way of communicating nonverbally. Her expression definitely said, "Look at that dumb dog chasing his tail."

I believe Newly was bored out of his gourd. He has no playmates except for an occasional hiss from the cat. We wrestle with Newly every chance we get, but that's not enough.

The dog has a lot of time on his paws and finds creative things to do. A favorite activity includes dragging concrete chunks, glass bottles and scrap lumber from under the house into the backyard. The yard is a showcase for many rawhide chew bones that have disinergrated because of his teething. He is definitely bored.

There are days when we end up chasing our tails and going in circles. Perhaps we are just bored.

Some folks may watch us go through our own mental contortions as they squint through life's window. What a show we must put on for people!

Boredom can come from too much concentration on ourselves and our inward thoughts. Sometimes we act like the world eagerly awaits to hear our thoughts and opinions on a variety of subjects.

Perhaps we need to listen more before we randomly

expound words of wisdom to an already overly opinionated sea of humanity. A passage from the Good Book reveals this wisdom: A fool takes no pleasure in understanding, but only expressing his opinion.

We often speak first, act second and think third. Will our words offend someone? What is their purpose? Do we open our mouths just to hear ourselves talk or to provide a place for our feet?

Back to the dog and cat tale. Thomasina really believes Newly is stupid for chasing his tail. However, Newly probably thinks all cats are a bit uppity. If the dog wants to chase his tail, snatch it and walk sideways, it's up to the dog. If the cat wants to be so haughty, she has that prerogative.

So, in the forthcoming years of a blissful life together, they will continue to be the animals God intended each one to be; differences and all.

We can celebrate together our own unique differences without chasing our tails, going in circles or running our mouths.

Life: 101 Taught By a Cat

People have pets for various reasons. A dog has always been my first choice for a pet.

As a youngster, one dog really became part of the family. Chumley, a white bull dog, resembled my late, great aunt, Miss Annie. Also, if he wore a bow tie, a derby and held a cigar between his teeth, Chumley could pass for Winston Churchill.

I never really cared for cats. They were fine for other people until – Dreyfuss.

This furry feline took up residence on Cross Street about the same time Amanda and I did. Perhaps he scooted in with the boxes and a large assortment of furniture.

Let me tell you about my first experience with a cat. My 8th grade science teacher, Eddie Miller, presented me with one. I always figured cats could take care of themselves in the house. Boy, was I wrong. This frisky feline surveyed my house and made deposits under the bed, in the bathroom sink and in the closet. After three days, this over-achiever found another home.

Amanda, the Mother Teresa of Stray Animals, loves cats. She has had several of them as pets and has tried to assure me that felines are all right.

I always felt that cats could never be trusted. They

seemed mysterious. I never felt comfortable or close to a cat. Dogs were warm and friendly, but cats were aloof and reserved, giving the appearance of being a little bit better than any of God's other creatures.

Learning to like and enjoy the presence of a feline in my house was an ordeal. It was like acquiring a taste for spinach. However, once I laid aside my own prejudice about cats, I was able to understand Dreyfuss as just one of many lovable animals. Cats are as cuddly as puppies, curious by nature and born adventurers. They love to take risks. Dreyfuss is one cat I'm glad I didn't miss.

Prejudging people through the lenses of past experiences sometimes hampers us from receiving a beautiful surprise. Everyone has to trust somebody at some point in their life.

We need to understand and practice a simple truth: *We may not be able to control life, but we can always control how we respond to life.*

Dreyfuss is not perfect. He left a little surprise in my shoe one morning. Amanda came to his defense by saying my shoe was the same size as the litter box and he was confused. Yeah, but I don't wear his litter box on my feet.

Cats are cats and dogs are dogs and people . . . well, we aren't perfect either. We, too, need a reassuring hug when we forget to use the litter box.

Goose Leaves Surprises in Car

Spring Lake Park is a favorite gathering spot for folks who live on both sides of Texarkana. Families still partake of picnic lunches under the trees.

In past years, people lined up to fill jugs with water from the park's natural spring. Now the water supply is condemned. Legend has it that the explorer De Soto stopped there for water.

Up-and-coming rock bands once gave free concerts at the park pavilions.

On most Friday and Saturday nights, cars are lined up around the small lake. When I was in high school, dating couples called this activity "watching underwater submarine races."

Feeding ducks is another favorite activity among Texarkansans. On Saturday or Sunday afternoons, parents would load their kids into the car and it's off to feed the hungry ducks and geese.

Each child rushed to the lake's edge, sack of stale bread in hand, and began tossing slices to the ducks. Soon parents would carefully demonstrate how to tear off a tiny piece to make it easier on the feathered friends.

One particular Saturday afternoon, Franz Baskett (a childhood buddy), his mother and I took a trip to feed the ducks. What transpired during the afternoon taught Franz and me a lesson about life and ducks.

We spent a couple of hours stuffing ducks with bread. Watching their table manners was interesting. Franz and I could identify with the famished fowls.

We noticed some were more aggressive than others. These devious birds would almost snatch the bread out of another's beak.

Some were shy, coming close only after the pushy ones failed to devour waterlogged crumbs. Still, others did not bother to come no matter how much we enticed them.

Our bread supply ran out. I cannot recall who came up the bright idea, but suddenly Franz and I were chasing geese.

Have you ever chased geese? It's not as easy as you think, even for limber kids. We had one thing on our mind – grabbing a gander. I believe it was Franz who finally nabbed one.

Our plan was to transport the goose home with us. The only way we could do this was to place our prisoner into the trunk of the car. We did and quickly shut the trunk.

On the ride back to his house, we talked about how neat it was to have a goose. We replayed the whole incident, word for word, all the way home.

As the trunk lid was opened, we were shocked to find our goose had left surprises inside. There were splatters of surprise on the top, on the sides and on the bottom of the trunk. There wasn't one inch of space that hadn't been surprised.

Needless to say, Mrs. Baskett was not a happy camper. I was just thankful it wasn't my mother's car.

Like the goose, we do not function well when we are trapped. Sometimes, we exist in emotional prisons with prison guards of pushy, manipulating people standing ready to contain us.

When feeling trapped in a life situation, we can make a mess of things. Obviously, the goose was not meant to be trapped in a trunk.

Our feathered friend was soon returned to the park where it probably lived a long life. However, from that day on, it may have felt a bit nervous around small boys with sacks of stale bread in their grubby little hands.

We are happier when we are free.

Brother Kills Sister at Mealtime

This is not just another furry cat tale. My cats, Thomasina and Jake, recently taught me a lesson in life. I didn't tell them because they would get the big head.

As we all know, cats have different personalities. Thomasina was a gift from Amanda when another cat, Dreyfus, decided to set out on the open road.

Thomasina was purchased from a pet store. She is a demanding, self-centered and self-serving feline. I suppose it's because she was pampered at the pet shop.

Jake came up the hard way. As a small kitten, he was found by a friend of Amanda's at a dumpster, fighting for survival.

The friend asked Amanda if she would give the cat a home. Of course, we would.

Jake is gentle by nature. He is unassuming and rarely gets upset when Thomasina takes advantage of his generosity.

On a particular afternoon, I noticed they needed food. I filled their dish and gave them a bowl of fresh water.

Jake heard the familiar sound of cat chow hitting the empty bowl and made graceful steps to the feast.

He huddled around the bowl and began eating. The back door opens and Thomasina (the cat can open the door by herself) sashays over to the bowl, pushes Jake away and begins to eat.

Jake hates conflict, but I could tell he was coming up with something as he intently watched Thomasina eat.

"I oughta kill her. But I'll going to kill her with kindness," Jake thought.

The next moment, Jake was licking the top of Thomasina's head almost to the point of forcing it into the bowl.

She got enough of that sort of kindness and left. Now Jake had the bowl all to himself. He would have shared the feast with her if Thomasina hadn't been so darn greedy. The lesson learned had to do with sharing, caring and working together.

Country humorist Jerry Clower has a sign hanging on a wall in his office which reads: *It's amazing what can be accomplished if it doesn't matter who gets the credit.*

An individual or a town has a great opportunity to accomplish much if these simple words are put into practice. This slogan may strike deep at the heart of dividedness among families and towns.

Why is it so important to some folks to receive credit for every little thing they do? Would it look good on a resume? Do they need one more appreciation plaque on their wall?

Appreciation is wonderful and we need to show our appreciation for others more often than we do. But, if that's the reason we are involved in projects, then we need to reevaluate ourselves.

In his day, St. Paul dealt with all sorts of people. He served as mediator between people who were fussing and fighting among themselves. His advice was, "You shall love your neighbor as yourself. But if you bite and devour one another, take heed that you are not consumed by one another."

Maybe Jake is right. Perhaps we can kill "them" with kindness, or at least wound them. Together much can be accomplished; divided, no one wins and dreams are never realized.

Life in Texarkana

*Texarkana: A city where the state boundary line
runs through the middle of the post office, where
Tigers and Razorbacks continue to fight in the fall
and where my childhood memories recall feelings
of love and moments of laughter.*

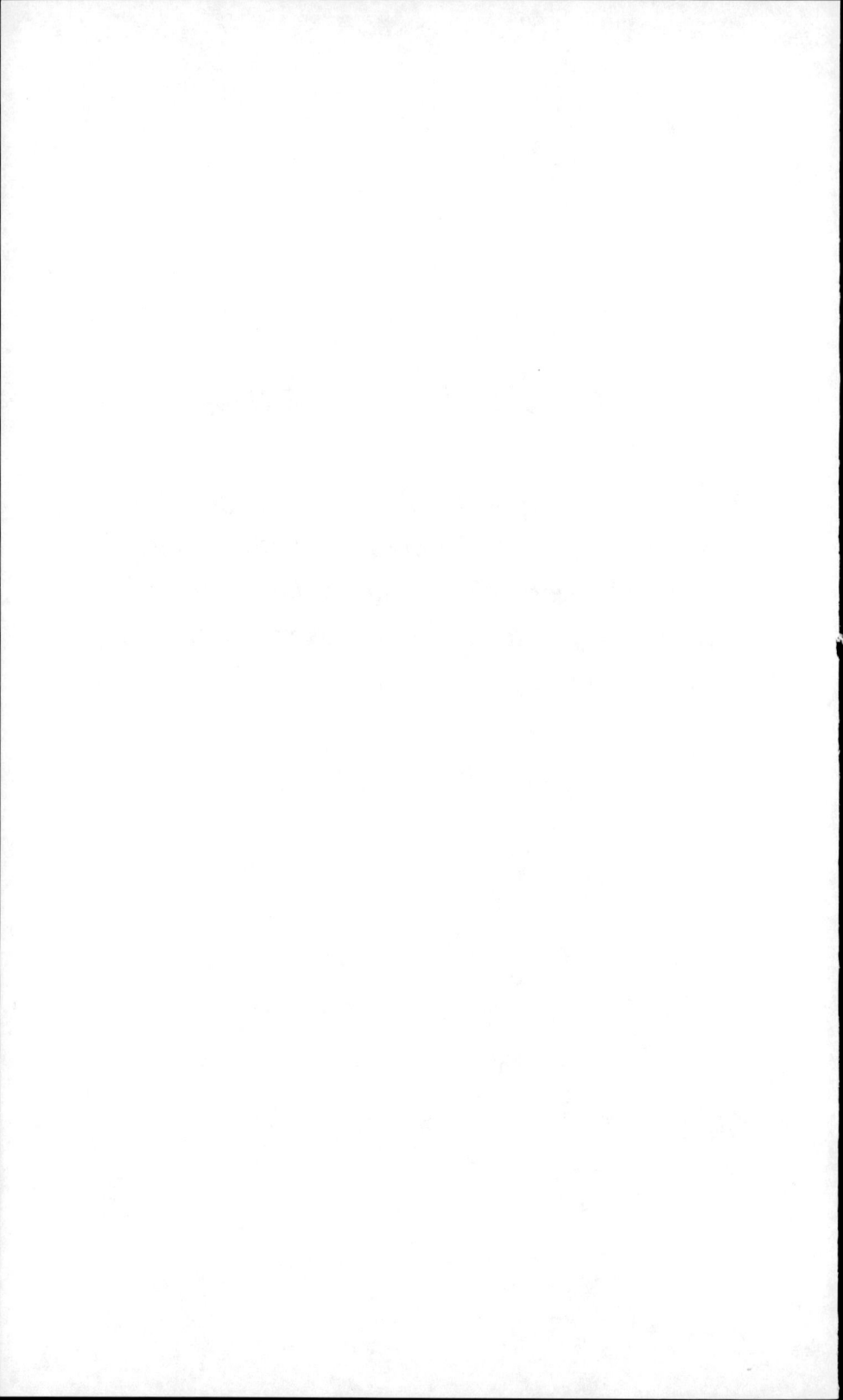

Woman Advocates Nudity

Shaving cream commercials that appear on the television screen will try almost anything to entice men to shave. Remember the blonde Norwegian bombshell who said, "Take it off," while striptease music played in the background? How many men decided to shave because of it?

One of the more memorable "rites of passage" experienced by young boys on the path to manhood is the first shave. At first glance, you would not think I would write a column on shaving. Basically, I do not like to shave. Just the area under my beard is enough for me. Besides, I like a beard and so does Amanda.

Young sons have grown up watching their fathers go through the early morning ritual of removing stubble from their faces. I was no exception.

My father would splash his face with Williams' 'Lectric Shave, rub it with a small towel and mow his beard with an electric razor.

One Christmas, I received a red, plastic toy electric razor. It had a black cord dangling from the bottom with a black suction cup attached to provide a realistic effect of hooking up to an imaginary electrical plug in.

I remember a classmate of mine, Allan Western, who

had been shaving since the sixth grade. With his black hair, he had a 4 o'clock shadow at the end of the school day.

By the ninth grade, it was time to get rid of my peach fuzz. One night I decided to shave. I walked into the bathroom and began the ritual. With the buzzing sound of the electric razor, I moved into another phase of my manhood.

I made the same weird facial expressions that accompany such practices. However, I did not count on an audience. I noticed my mother's face peering around the corner to watch this historic event.

Shaving technology has taken great strides to make this morning ritual more pleasant for us guys. Double-edged razors, with a numbered band to raise or lower the blade's sharpness, have hit the markets making it less of a hassle to shave.

We all use more shaving cream than we need. It seems to grow in our hands. Most of it goes down the drain.

Shaving gel became a norm which aided us in conserving shaving cream.

Several years ago, I purchased a shaving mug, shaving soap and a shaving brush to apply the lather. I really like it better. No more messy hands filled with excess shaving cream.

All in all, shaving one's face is a skill learned after several hours of practice. Boys are not born to shave. I wonder how many pints of blood are shed annually because of those little nicks? My face has seen its share of small pieces of tissue paper stuck to those minor cuts.

Maybe this is why I am beginning to see a few more bearded faces than I did in past years.

Little Brown Jug Brings Relief

The saying goes, "You don't miss your water 'till your well runs dry." Just tell us we can't water our lawns, wash our cars or take a dip in the nearest swimming pool because there is a water shortage, and we will give you all kinds of reasons why we must take care of these watery tasks now. Even kids, who normally gulp down several two-liter bottles of Coke, want a glass of ice cold water to quench their thirst.

Amanda and I are Dr. Pepper people. We should buy stock in the company. However, I've enjoyed drinking more water than I was accustomed to before we married. We keep a glass jug of water in the ice box at all times so that it is accessible when one of us wants a swig. A container of water is located next to the milk in refrigerators in several homes across America. Water is good for humans. Our bodies are mostly made up of this stuff.

There is another twist to this liquid refreshment. Sometimes, Amanda adds a slice of lemon to her water. This recipe was passed down to her by a good friend. She suggested I try it and I did, although, I secretly added some sugar. After asking for a sip, she exclaimed, "This is lemonade!" "Sure it is. I thought that's what you had in mind," I said. After correcting the error, I have come to enjoy a refreshing glass of lemon water. Don't laugh. It's the best thirst quencher going.

My great-aunt, Miss Annie, had a jug containing different contents. When she moved in for her annual visit with me and my parents, her two month stay often felt like two years. One of the important items she always purchased was a jug of A&P brand prune juice.

This potion was packaged in a tall, brown, rectangular glass jug. Its shape fit perfectly into the side door of our Coldspot refrigerator. You can bet this concoction was finished soon, because Miss Annie insisted on being regular and right on schedule.

My mother washed the empty brown jug thoroughly, filled it with water and placed it in the side door of the ice box. Remembering the prune juice, I didn't much care for water from that particular container.

Uncle Harold and Aunt Lois live around the corner from my parents in Texarkana. As I recall, a green, glass water jug held a prominent place in their refrigerator. Over the years, it has been replaced by a long, thin plastic container with a protruding water spout.

Technology has taken away some of the little pleasures, like washing empty fruit juice jugs, peeling off the labels and filling them with water. Manufacturers have given us refrigerators with ice dispensers on the outside next to a water tap. I like the old-fashioned glass jug idea better. It's easier to get a swig, it has more character and the water tastes better.

Some things just can't get any better, only more complicated. Maybe Thoreau was right when he wrote the immortal words "Simplify, simplify, simplify."

No Need to Explain

I remember, or perhaps I remember my parents telling me, of the time I ran through Aunt Lois' house with a wooden yardstick in search of a dragon to slay. I found an appropriate dragon to kill – her washing machine. The battle was long fought and very bloody, as far as fire-breathing washing machines go.

What Aunt Lois said to me has followed me all my life. She asked, "Why did you do that?"

At age four, I wasn't clever enough to come up with a good reason. I just said, "I don't know." From that moment on, I've felt a nervous compulsion to explain everything.

Do you know what I mean?

Life explainers come from many different backgrounds. They are wealthy and poor. Some are well-educated and others think *Reader's Digest* is a person who reads while he eats. We are everywhere.

Life explainers typically feel it's their fault for just about everything, from the way the economy is going to the reason for the high rate of high school dropouts. They feel guilty for speeding and slow down when a highway patrol car passes them on the interstate.

The most evident characteristic of the life explainer is that they explain their very lives away. When asked, "Why did you do that?" The immediate response is a very long and drawn out dissertation filled to the brim with as many excuses as Carter's got liver pills.

The Good Book is right when it says "let your yes, be yes and your no, be no." Don't try to explain everything, we lose our potency as a person when we do so.

Life explainers are also People Pleasers. They want to satisfy everyone – even at their own expense. They want everybody to like them, so they try to please. The problem is that everyone is not going to like us no matter what we do.

People Pleasers are focused on this need to please others. Consequently, they end up not knowing what they believe, who they really are, or what they want to do. They have tried to be what everyone wanted them to be for so long that they have acquired a chameleon image that changes with every situation. They seek to be accepted.

There is a line from Rick Nelson's song *Garden Party* which says, "You can't please everyone, so you got to please yourself." People Pleasers can't identify with these words because they believe everyone else is more important than they are.

People Pleasers hide their true feelings behind masks of politeness and martyrdom. Will we ever learn to be true to ourselves?

A scene from the movie *Network* shows us a has-been television talk show host emerging as a real person after his show's ratings begin to drop drastically. He starts saying what he feels rather than what others want him to say.

He tells people in the viewing audience to get mad. He demands that everyone go to their windows, stick their head out, and yell, "I'm mad as hell and I'm not going to take it anymore!" He asks, "Now don't you feel better?"

Sometimes we need to get angry enough to do what we need to do. I don't mean we ought to "pitch a fit." Fits get us nowhere fast.

But we need to get angry at ourselves for allowing people to run over us, allowing people to use us as door mats, allowing people to determine our lives for us and allowing ourselves to believe we are just not good enough.

That's a good reason to get angry, isn't it? I know. I know. You don't have to say it. We aren't supposed to get angry. It just isn't polite. However, anger can be a positive power when used in a creative, rather than destructive way.

We ridicule the politicians for being political. Then we turn around and act the same way by saying what we think others want us to say instead of what we really mean.

Our lives are as precious as pearls to each one of us. Treat you life as a fine gem sparkling in the brilliant light of each new day.

One more paraphrased word from the Good Book –
Don't throw your pearls before a herd of uncaring, self-
centered, and slobbering pigs. They will trample all over
you.

You are a priceless gem. There is no need to explain.
Start shining!

What's on the Boob Tube?

What's on television tonight?

This was my main concern while growing up. You see, I am from the "boob tube baby" generation.

In 1957, my family had one black and white television set. Dad controlled most of the viewing, but Saturday mornings were mine. I ate my oatmeal topped with crumbled bacon as fast as I could in order to watch The Lone Ranger, Sky King, My Friend Flicka, Roy Rogers, Dale Evans and Gabby Hayes.

As an only child with both parents working, the television became my best friend. I explored outer space. I fought with the cowboys and the Indians. I laughed with Woody Woodpecker, Deputy Dawg, and Mighty Mouse. The television was a fantastic companion.

My dad and I had many discussions about who was going to watch what and when.

I remember vividly the night an Elvis Presley movie was coming on the television. I wanted to watch it and my dad wanted to watch something else. A very heated discussion followed.

Soon after that incident, I had my very own black and white magic box. It was a used one, but that didn't matter. The lid lifted to expose all the controls. I thought I had died and gone to heaven.

One night in 1964, the air was thick with anticipation. Curtains were drawn, lights were out, hot dogs and popcorn were served as the television show, The Wild, Wild, West came into focus. It was like being at the picture show. The grass was really green and the horses were really brown, just as in real life. My dad had bought a new television and the words "living color" entered our living room.

Back then, there was access to only three channels. It was before the advent of cable television and satellite dishes.

As television technology increased, so did our waistlines. We moved from the dinner table to TV trays in order to view favorite programs at suppertime. This was highlighted by the remote control. We stopped getting exercise by having to get up and change channels by manual control. There are very few of the P-RCA (pre-remote control age) still around today. Folks sat in their recliners with a zombie-like trance spread across their faces. Their thumbs rapidly pressing the channel changer as bits and pieces, blurs and colors passed by on the screen.

Our lives began being directed by an intellectually stimulating magazine called the TV Guide, one of the most widely read magazines on the market today. People quit going out, sitting on the front porch and reading because it would interfere with one of "their" shows. Relationships were going down the tubes. People were being asked to call back after a certain show was over.

Technology has now provided the ultimate machine, the famous VCR (video cassette recorder). We don't have to miss another soap opera, mini-series or late, late movie. We can record them and watch them later. I've always wanted to watch "Late Night with David Letterman" at 7 in the morning. With the VCR, we can rent movies, prop our feet up and enjoy them in the comfort of our own home.

I confess, I once was a "boob tube addict," but not any more. I found the cure. When a person comes into your life, I mean a very special person, you realize the television just isn't as exciting as being with that special someone.

I have found a special person in Amanda. We enjoy talking about anything from politics and religion, to music and old houses. We laugh more than any two people I know. We would rather take brisk walks together than plug into the television. She has given me many moments of laughter, love and joy.

You find comfort with people, not things. Maybe it's time to change TV channels. Or maybe just turn it off.

"There's not much on tonight. What do you want to do?"

"I don't know. What do you want to do?"

"I don't know. It doesn't matter to me."

"Why don't we just talk with each other."

"Do you remember how?"

"Let's see. How does it go again?"
"Oh yeah ... How was your day?"

Birthday Candles Snuffed Out

I could have handled the situation a bit differently, but when you are in the first grade, you have a limited amount of diplomatic resources to call upon.

It amazes me that I remember the incident at all. The details that led up to the outburst are still fuzzy. However, I vividly recall my actions.

This very special day took 364 days to arrive. Plans for the big occasion were made and carried out with great care. The day was Oct. 21, 1958 – my sixth birthday.

This particular birthday celebration was the first time I had a party at a location other than my own home. (The feeling is similar to the joy I felt the first time I brought my lunch to school rather than eating the entrees in the school cafeteria.) My parents had secured a large room in a community building. Classmates from St. James Episcopal School and friends from the neighborhood were invited to the gala event.

A few party games were played leading up to the main event of tearing into the presents. (It is important at this point for the reader to remember that I received a pair of simulated, pearl handled cowboy six-shooters with a holster as one of my gifts.)

After the "oohs and aahs" subsided, the worst rendition of *Happy Birthday* ever heard by human ears was performed. It is customary for the birthday honoree to endure the embarrassment of this song before ice cream and cake can be served. For some of us, the singing of this song is equal to the sound of fingernails scraping down a chalkboard.

All six candles were lit. I inhaled as deeply as I could. I had enough wind in my lungs to launch the Santa Maria.

Suddenly, out of nowhere, Ray Abernathy jumped up and blew out every single candle on my birthday cake. He had stolen the only chance for my wish coming true.

In a rage, I grabbed one of the six-shooters and wacked him on top of his flat-top-haircut head. Small drops of blood trickled from the cut.

Here, my memory does fail me, but feelings of remorse and sympathy for Ray soon followed the incident. I was sorry I hurt him. It was a natural knee-jerk, impulsive response.

I cannot say exactly why I hit him. However, the late Jim Croce told us in a song that there are a few things you just don't do. You don't tug on Superman's cape, spit into the wind, pull the mask off the Lone Ranger and . . . you don't blow out the candles of someone's birthday cake.

A birthday is a big deal when you are six. As the

years accumulate, they become less significant. In fact, the exact number of years one has occupied space on this planet are sometimes forgotten.

If you asked Ray today why he blew out the candles, he probably wouldn't remember the incident or would say, "I don't know why."

Memories of this event has not damaged our relationship. So much has happen to us since that October day that any feelings of hurt or embarrassment have faded over the years.

Most of us have experienced similar incidents in our "coming of age" years. Some have been more tragic than this one. Still we wonder why they happened at all.

For your next birthday, why not give yourself a gift. Take the difficult memories that time has not faded, place them in a box, tie it up, and discard it!

Those Bubble Gum Days

I once enjoyed chewing bubble gum, or any kind of chewing gum for that matter, but that was before these darn braces were cemented to my teeth.

The sweet, sugary smell that drifted from newly opened wrappers of Super Bubble, Bazooka and Double Bubble is only a faded memory. My buddies and I would chew gum until our jaws ached and then chew some more.

A reward of bubble gum always followed a haircut during my childhood. The smell of Butch Wax and bubble gum filled the barbershop.

Back in those early days, the gum was bigger than it is today. The large amount of sugar is missing, along with its evidence of white powder that smudged our fingers and caked around the corners of our mouth.

Today, when a piece of bubble gum is unwrapped, our nostrils aren't treated to that sweet aroma. In fact, one can only get a hint that it's really bubble gum.

Let me say at this point that the bubble gum is only part of the joy. The other joyful part came when we read these small comics neatly folded inside the wrapper.

I remember a song that asked whether our chewing gum lost its flavor on the bedpost overnight. The song sounds silly now, but there was a lot of truth to those words. I have been known to stick my gum on books to save it until the next day.

Hard sticks of bubble gum that broke in pieces were found inside a new pack of baseball cards. (I have no idea where they found these terrible tasting excuses for bubble gum.)

Collecting baseball cards is big business. I call it the poor man's stock market. Baseball card companies know this. The value of, say, a Ken Griffey Jr. card is decreased when stained by bubble gum. This is why sticks of bubble gum are rarely found inside a new pack today.

Bubble gum chewing as a youngster was a dangerous time for me, especially when I fell asleep at night with a wad of gum still in my mouth.

I remember waking up one morning wondering where the gum I went to bed with had gone. I soon discovered it was matted in my hair.

My mother placed ice cubes on the sticky mess (to harden it) and then cut the gum from my hair.

Blowing a bubble can also be hazardous. On many occasions I have blown a gigantic bubble with the aid of about five pieces of bubble gum crammed inside my mouth.

Suddenly, from out of nowhere, someone's finger pierced my artwork, splattering it all over my face. Another application of ice was needed. (This was before stickless gum.)

There are also aspects that tend to annoy folks. Just recently, I opened my car door to enter a business and was stuck to the pavement. Some gum-chewing airhead had decided to throw away his gum near the front of the store.

All we have are the memories of when bubble gum was real. There is no future in "sticking" to the past. Someone would only "burst" our bubble.

No Hitt Game

That July night was humid. I adjusted my Little League baseball cap, wiped sweat from my forehead, wound up and pitched my best fast ball. "Strike three. You're out of there," yelled the umpire. Recently, Amanda found the baseball I used to pitch that no-hitter. "July 7, 1964" was clearly written on its cover.

I went to play some baseball with my son at that same field during one of my visits to Texarkana. It had been purchased by the high school and there seemed to be more buildings erected at the site than when I was a boy.

A brief aside here about homerun hitting. If you have ever hit a homerun, you know the feeling and recall the sound as the bat connects with the ball. During one such moment, I remember my feet didn't move from the batter's box. I knew it was a homer. When the ball dropped over the centerfield fence, excitement welled up inside me. I wanted to whip around the bases like the wind. However, I knew the proper etiquette after one hits a homerun. You don't run around the bases. A gentle jog is more appropriate. That's what I did. I felt like Mickey Mantle.

Back to the no-hitter. After all these years, the yellowed newspaper article from the *Texarkana Gazette* is still taped in a scrapbook at my parent's home. The discolored clipping carries the headline: **HALEY HURLS NO-HITTER** . Those words have a particular ring and rhythm. At least they do to me. I've had them memorized for 25 years.

I have written some baseball reports for *The Benton Courier* sports pages. I discovered a wide assortment of adjectives used to describe certain plays. Words like slammed, crushed, squeezed and smothered are frequently used to bring the actual feeling of the game to the reader.

Sports writers have a unique flair when it comes to their stories. The *Texarkana Gazette* sports writer painted this picture: "Thomas Haley pitched a no-hitter and struck out 12. Haley also contributed a homerun as Hedrick Electric blitzed Offenhauser 7-0 in Little League action."

I like that word "blitzed." It told the story.

In a small town, people will do outstanding things that make its way across the pages of the local newspaper. They are celebrities, if only for a brief moment.

I dreamed of playing in the major leagues. Little did I know that I would earn a living by the written word. The date and score printed on the baseball was accompanied by the words **"No Hitt Game."** I didn't have an editor in 1964 to correct my misspelled words.

Oh well. As in life, you win a few, lose a few, and some get rained out.

Reading Isn't Always Believing

What you see isn't always exactly what you get.

Advertisements in comic books always caught my eye as a child. One stated, "250 Civil War Soldiers for only $1."

I couldn't wait to get some money to send off for all these soldiers. I got my dollar, carefully cut out the order blank and stuck it in the mailbox.

Beginning that afternoon, I waited for the mailman. I hate to wait now, but at 8 years of age, waiting even 20 minutes was eternity. Finally, the long-anticipated day came.

How could 250 Civil War soldiers fit into that little box? I thought, "This can't be all of them. Maybe there will be other boxes coming." I opened the box and my heart sank to my feet. Yes, there were 250 soldiers – all paper-thin, red or blue plastic ones. I took out the ad and looked one more time. What I got was not what was portrayed in the comic book.

This was my first lesson in the adage: "What you see is <u>not</u> always what you get."

I once had a hobby of writing down those slogans churches use on signs or in phone books to describe who they are or what they offer.

Here are a few:

* **The Church with the Red Doors.** I guess to the fashion-minded person this church would be enticing, but says nothing of the church.

* **The Church that's Interested in Little Folks.** Does this mean that if you are over 5 feet tall they are not interested in you? Still this says nothing about the church.

* **Our Fellowship is Patterned After the New Testament Church.** Wait a minute! The New Testament Church does not indicate something appealing to me. In that day and time martyr was their middle name. I, for one, need the convenience of indoor toilets, a luxury the New Testament church didn't enjoy.

* **Enjoy the Small Church Options.** This sounds like a small group gathered to negotiate with larger churches. It smells of developing political prowess and says nothing about the church.

* **Independent-Fundamental-Premillennial.** The writing is on the wall. If you like to be by yourself, rigid, and believe the reign of Christ is happening now before the last trumpet sound, then this is the place for you. I once knew someone who was a panmillennial, which means in the end, everything will pan out.

* **You Are Important To Us.** Everybody wants to be and feel important. Usually, after going over your

pledge card and seeing the amount written in the blank, you become less important. What is warm in the beginning can easily become cold as ice.

* **Helping You Serve Him.** This is probably one of the most honest slogans I have run across. The catch word is serve. Most people want to be served rather than do the serving themselves.

Those 250 Civil War soldiers marched their way into my mailbox, but weren't well received.

I have heard this description of a person: The deeper you dig the more shallow he is.

Some things are not what they appear to be.

By the way, I've got some land in Florida . . .

Popcorn and Cash Registers

Certain smells can conjure up a bouquet of memories for us. If we listen very closely, there are distinct sounds which can bring to mind a cornucopia of remembrances.

I remember Saturdays in Texarkana and going downtown to the "Dime Store." This store actually had items from a nickel to a dollar.

It was a magical place for me. I can still smell the aroma of freshly popped popcorn smothered in butter greeting me as I entered this wonderful kingdom. I was enticed to venture on a marvelous journey, without the aid of a map, in search of precious treasures.

I remember going up and down the aisles with two quarters burning away at the material in my pants pocket. My parents and relatives always told me about money burning a hole in my pocket. I separated the two quarters for fear the friction from the silver would spark a flame. However, the only burning was the immediate question, "What can I buy today?"

After I had exhausted every conceivable idea of what to buy, I would finally make a decision.

One day I bought a yo-yo and two packs of baseball cards. I carefully placed my loot on the checkout counter.

There was always an older lady standing there. She would look at me as if to say, "Those are some wise choices. You will have fun with them." She could see the pride beaming from my face.

I recall the unmistakable and unforgettable noise of the cash register as she hit the keys with the grace of a concert pianist. There was a rhythm to each stroke as she tapped the buttons and with each note played, a numbered metal card popped up like a duck in a shooting gallery.

Those Saturdays were more relaxed, more magical, and more memorable than today. One could stroll around, enjoy a bag of popcorn and watch other people being drawn to the candy counter by the fragrance.

I don't smell that smell anymore. It left with the dime stores, never to return except maybe in this writing.

I don't hear the alluring sound of the cash register. It has been replaced with beeps, buzzes, and electronic glitzes.

The cashiers are much younger now. There is a certain amount of character missing.

Recently, while I was standing in a checkout line, a young cashier was nearing hysterics because her register wouldn't work. Her awful dilemma was having to add sales tax and make change. She had never done that before. The automatic cash register had always performed that function. It had only been a matter of pushing buttons.

Her body was shaking and her voice quivering as

anxious people began lining up at her counter. Customers had their baskets stacked and were in a hurry to get out. They were getting very impatient because this cashier couldn't deal with real money, real change, and real thinking.

Some things remain the same.

The need to use our minds and not be dependent on electronic devices to give us answers is very important. If you don't use it, you can lose it. Maybe that is why the young cashier was losing hers.

Sounds and smells come and go. Dime stores are replaced with larger variety stores. Cashiers get younger.

No matter what mode of technology, the feeling of self-confidence and the warmth of people to people are incredible gifts that never go out of style or become obsolete.

Can you get this yo-yo string untangled for me?

Memories Linger After Funeral

In most cases, we are never quite ready to lose a loved one to death. We are sometimes better prepared to accept this event than at other times, but the sting is still there.

On the first day of April, an early morning phone call from my mother informed me that my uncle had died.

Uncle Harold had danced on the edge of death many times before; however, this day had been his last waltz.

Relatives and friends, whom I haven't seen in several years, gathered throughout the small house on Hickory Street in Texarkana. Food seems to abound whenever families and friends come together, even at funerals. My father sampled desserts at least twice and always said he shouldn't. That's a tradition.

We laughed and talked about our past experiences together and caught up on what had happened in our lives since we had last seen each other.

After the funeral service, Amanda and I rode with "Dot" and my parents to Hillcrest Cemetery. Dot, a lifelong friend of my mother, is a west Texas character. God broke the mold with her.

As the funeral procession began its long journey to

the graveside, I noticed motorists pulling onto the shoulder of the road to pay their respects. As we passed one corner, I observed a bearded man dressed in soiled work clothes kindly take off his hat and bow his head. He didn't know my uncle, but I bet he knows the sadness of death.

Along the highway, I saw abandoned buildings, new ones under construction and an old familiar friend – a giant, stuffed rabbit sitting in front of a gas station. The sight of that rabbit brought back memories.

When I was a youngster, my family would take an occasional Sunday afternoon trip to the cemetery and sometimes stop at that same gas station. I would climb upon the creatures's furry back and into the saddle. "Ride 'em, Rabbit." (Somewhere a photograph depicting this event exists.)

The procession approached the cemetery. My father was quick to point out the rundown, ratty-looking shacks that once served as a motel. They are now used as low rent housing.

Figures emerged from screenless doors left open due to lack of air conditioning. I wondered how often they had witnessed a funeral procession. My eyes focused back to the cemetery's entrance and an old family marker which had always produced a smile for me. Carved on the large stone was the name "O'Rear." Oh, really?

I couldn't erase the impoverished scene from my

mind. Destitution, with hollow eyes and lean bodies, stood in the doorways of the motel-shacks. The graves and the people in poverty. I pondered the difference; the dead and the living dead located across the highway from each other.

I was brought back to reality when my father reminded all of us that our family plot lies next to the gravesites belonging to one of the wealthiest families in the city.

"One thing for sure, we are all equal when we die," I said.

Somewhere, Uncle Harold, with a foursome, is about to tee off on a new course. After his drive, he will walk down the fairway with his unforgettable stroll while someone like me is following behind carrying his clubs. I'll miss him.

We grieve, cry, remember, wonder, laugh and continue with the day to day process of living. Life does go on.

Love People, Not Things

Suicide, at any age, is an alarming fact of life. It seems that this tragedy increases in number among youth with each new year. Questions, questions and more questions seem to hover around us as we wonder what causes people to end their lives in such a violent manner.

I delivered my first funeral sermon in shock; not because it was my first, but because it was for a very close boyhood friend, Wayne Birts.

Even though it has been a decade since his death, I can still remember the sound of the phone ringing. The voice of Jim Hudson, another close friend, gently told me that Wayne had shot himself and died. I slid down the wall into a slumped position and wept. "Why?" I asked. No answers came; only more questions.

I am very close to Wayne's family. Although I hadn't seen them in years, I felt honored when they asked me to preach the service. It was extremely difficult for me. Even today, tears become evident when I recall those tense, griping moments.

The church was important to Wayne. We both grew up in it and participated in every aspect. However, at that time, the church was not answering our questions. Wayne drifted away from it and I drifted into the ministry with the hope of making some changes.

The church will not change until the people within the church change. Some of the changes will hopefully include proclaiming and living out the message that people need to be accepted for who they are and not who we want them to be.

Everyone of us is a child of God – special; yet we are all different. We need to discover the person we want to be and be that person. Dream our dreams. We have everything within our grasp to accomplish this task if we believe in ourselves instead of what others believe about us.

We should let go of our need to control people. Let's control ourselves first. It is urgent that we learn to accept and understand people, rather than judge and condemn.

Constant ridicule will ultimately cause us to alienate people. If they feel separated from life's mainstream of activities, folks get scared and loose hope. This aloneness and hopelessness can have an adverse affect on us all.

I'm really not stuck in the 60s, but that historical time should be remembered for more than just long hair, beads and blue jeans. It was an attitude about life. It was a time of trying to understand each other. A time to build bridges of understanding rather than walls around closed minds. It was a time to care for the environment and the civil rights of all people. It was loving the unlovable. A time to share and give (or at least it was a goal).

It was a time to lift up the idea of letting go of material things and trying to hold on to each other. Even though we proclaimed acceptance of others in the 60s, it was not widely practiced in most of our lives.

Someone has said that the 90s are the 60s all over again. I tend to agree with this observation. Well, the issues and actions have a familiar sound: illegal drugs, environmental protection, protests, getting involved, taking a stand, questioning the status quo and authorities, attacking greed, saving animal life and, ultimately, all of life. We need to bring back the 60s attitude.

Today's parents of teenagers are the children of the 60s. Some understand their children because they understand themselves. Others cannot understand their children because they have lost touch with who they are or lost who they were.

Whether Wayne lost touch with himself, felt alienated, or had suffered a hurt that was too painful to endure, I don't know. However, I do know this; it is high time we work on accepting people and their different personalities before some of us lose all hope. Maybe the time has come to learn what it means to be a human being rather than a gold nugget with ears.

Families Full of Funny Folks

We all have them. Generations tell and retell their stories at family gatherings. Some are more colorful than others. They are called "relatives."

Memorable ones in all families include the miser who is so tight with his money that his shoes squeak, the idiot cousin who babbles constantly, the rich uncle who invites himself for lengthy stays with other relatives, the aunt who never tells her age but everyone believes they know, the unmarried niece who seems a little odd and the eccentric uncle who collects everything from buffalo chips to antique trash cans.

You can pick flowers, your friends and even your nose, but you can't pick your relatives.

My late great-aunts were sisters in Tennessee. Both women were born of the same mother and father, yet, they were as different as night and day.

Aunt Lillian Bates, the giver, loved life. She had caring and kindness in her touch. Those warm hands squeezed every drop out of life. When she and her relatives moved to Arizona, a bit of Tennessee traveled with them. In Tucson, their yard was the only one on the block with real grass. The rest of the neighborhood had yards decorated with green gravel.

At 92, she returned to Clarksville, Tennessee, for a visit. As she stepped off a curb, a car struck her. The hospital report indicated no broken bones or internal injuries. (This is a miracle in itself.) However, the doctor said he would have to remove the toes on her left foot. Aunt Lillian humorously replied,"Well, that's alright. That's five toes I won't have to trim."

Aunt Lillian gave to life without asking anything in return. A story was written about her in a Tucson newspaper naming her "grandmother of her neighborhood."

Her sister, Miss Annie Neblett, the taker, acted as if life owed her something. She expected the world and everyone in it to revolve around her wishes. Nothing or nobody had better bother her routine.

Her breakfast consisted of a bowl of cornflakes, followed by a piece of unbuttered toast carefully placed in an empty bowl and topped with a poached egg. She always had a glass of prune juice and a cup of Sanka. (Perked coffee kept her awake. She might miss her afternoon beauty nap.)

Opinions dripped from Miss Annie's mouth like drops of water from a leaky faucet. In fact, this feisty little woman was so outspoken that she was unofficially elected Mayor of Seventh Street in Clarksville by neighbors who dealt with her on a daily basis.

Miss Annie took from life and Aunt Lillian gave to

life. I loved them both for different reasons because there is a bit of their traits in us all.

The Tennessee sisters have passed on to their reward and heaven will never be the same again. When the news of Miss Annie's passing reached God's ears, a hush fell over the masses of angels. He knew his work was cut out for Him. She will probably rearrange the Pearly Gates and patrol the streets of gold offering advice to Michael and St. Peter.

However, I'm sure there were joyous sounds all around and smiles awaiting Aunt Lillian at Heaven's Door when she died. She will assure everyone they are loved and cared for even in the presence of "the Mayor."

Two types of people exist on this planet – givers and takers. They come in all shapes, sizes and colors.

Givers have a flaw. When one gives and gives and receives nothing in return, they are vulnerable to greedy takers.

Takers usually have a deep, empty feeling when they are honest with themselves. They are never quite satisfied.

How are you feeling?

Front Porch Gatherings

Kitchens are a favorite gathering spot in most homes. How large would your kitchen be compared to the rest of the rooms if you designed your dream house?

My parent's home in Texarkana is a modest two bedroom, one bath house with a combination living room and dining room. Their kitchen is relatively small compared to the other rooms, but it's a gathering place for relatives and guests.

A round oak table serves as the centerpiece. Family problems have been worked out as members sat around its curves. Heads were bowed as morning devotionals were read. Most of all, some of the best home cooked meals were served and devoured on this blessed piece of furniture.

Most of us have our own architectural prejudices when it comes to planning our dream houses. Some insist on enormous space in the bathrooms while others need large areas for dens.

Over the years, family dens have replaced the front porch. I remember days of sitting on porches and visiting with friends in Texarkana, Arkansas; Clarksville, Tennessee; and Macon, Missouri. At some point, people added dens, closed their curtains and plugged into a television set.

Neighbors never became neighbors because they were rarely seen.

In some neighborhoods, however, people are actually walking and talking with each other again. Gradually, front porches are being erected.

I believe America has been watching the classic reruns of *The Andy Griffith Show*. We have all watched as Andy and Barney gorge themselves on one of Aunt Bea's famous suppers and then retreat to the front porch, sprawl out in a chair and rest their stomachs. Often, Barney (who appeared to have never gained any weight over the years) would pat his stomach and provide a personal commentary about this meal being the best yet.

A notable piece of furniture, the porch swing, is showcased on Andy's front porch.

Some of the town folk, like Floyd (the barber), Goober or Gomer (from the gas station) or, perhaps, Emmett (Mr. Fix It) would stroll by and stop for a chat.

A cool night breeze rustled the hedge and all was well in Mayberry. Ah, such simple pleasures.

An American dream is to build a house with enough square footage to get lost in. Perhaps one reason people crave enormous houses is to get away from each other.

America, we need to get out more, talk with each other, walk around the block, purchase a round oak table and begin to communicate with each other over a plate of turnip greens and cornbread.

Perhaps we need to remodel our homes with the addition of a front porch, acquire a porch swing and enjoy the moments.

Mischief in the Afternoon

As a child, I suppose one could have called me a "latch-key" kid, but at the time I would not have known what you were talking about.

My parents' finances dictated the need for both of them to hold down jobs.

Before I stayed by myself after school, I had the middle class equivalent to a Southern-styled English nanny. Her name was Dimples. She was a tall, very large, black woman. One could describe her as 400 pounds of hungry. The sun's rays were reflected off her gold teeth when she grinned or laughed.

Every once in a while, Dimples would bring out her small tin of snuff. Her fingers would automatically pinch an appropriate amount and place it inside her bottom lip, as she had done many times before.

I loved Dimples. She was an unforgettable character in my life.

The second nanny was an older woman, Mrs. Gurley. She was gentle, but seemed a bit frail to me. (After Dimples, most anybody would have looked frail.) At that time, everyone who was over 20 years old looked that way to me.

Mrs. Gurley was a fine cook. Her homemade biscuits would melt in your mouth. They were the best.

I began staying home alone at about age 12. Those afternoons proved to be ripe for a little mischief. Ideas danced in my head as I had time on my hands. These moments were helpful in pursuing a variety of projects.

On one occasion, I decided the dog house needed a new coat of paint. I could not locate a paint brush so I improvised with a rag.

Aqua was the only color of paint I could find around the house. I assumed the dog would enjoy a bit more color to his abode.

If memory serves me well, I do not think I changed into work clothes. After the paint job, I could not find the paint thinner so I cleaned up in the kitchen sink. Telltale evidence remained on the back door. After that little project, I did not paint anymore.

To really be authentic playing Army, a soldier needed a foxhole dug in the backyard. I dug one. I made a tent frame and nailed one of my mother's favorite white crocheted bed spreads to it.

The tent was placed over the hole and just under a wild cherry tree that housed hundreds of "army worms." I wanted to exterminate the enemy so I made a torch and burned them out. Some of the flaming rags from the torch dropped onto the bedspread. I recall my butt being set on fire after my mother came home from work.

Another foxhole was dug. It quickly became a swimming pool after I hit the water line during the digging. I am sure I got it in the end.

Sometimes we do not think about consequences while we are involved in a particular project. We possess tunnel vision. All we can see is what we are doing at the time.

Mistakes are made. The only good that comes from them is that we learn not to try that one again. Believe me, I have learned from my mistakes. Well, at least from some of them.

Life in the South

In the South, we work hard and we play hard. We are elected to public offices. Some driveways have a pickup truck parked and ready for Bubba to start her up. We believe in education, but really prefer that one doesn't flaunt too much "book learnin'."

Cheeseburgers From Paradise

Three things seem to make up what we consider All American – Mom, apple pie and baseball.

I offer one more symbol of Americana – the homemade, old-fashioned cheeseburger.

Hey, I'm not talking about the fast food variety. (Sometimes I wonder about a meat patty shaped in a perfect square.)

There is a certain style and character involved in cooking a "real" cheeseburger just like Mom's. Never are any two patties made in the same identical way. Sort of like snowflakes and fingerprints. Each one is different.

Recently, I called my favorite mamma-in-law and asked if she could spare some slices of luncheon meat slapped between two pieces of bread. I had two interviews scheduled in her neck-of-the-woods, one before and one immediately after lunchtime. Before I knew it, she had invited me to partake of one of her famous "Gram" burgers. Amanda told me how delicious they are. I could tell she was a bit jealous.

The first interview seemed to drag on as visions of cheeseburgers danced in my head. High noon finally arrived and not a minute too soon.

After my first bite, all my palatal desires were fulfilled. Homemade french fries adorned the side of my plate, completing my cheeseburger paradise.

"Does Mr. Tummy want another one?" Mamma Betty asked with a grin. She knew what the answer would be.

I always want a second helping at Betty's Bar and Grill. I may not need it, but I always want it. Her homemade dumplins', fried chicken and banana puddin' should also be considered All-American. That's another menu. Back to cheeseburgers.

Recently, Amanda had a craving for a "real" cheeseburger. My favorite daddy-in-law had told Amanda and me about Loy's Snack Shop just off Interstate 30, at the Sevier Street exit in Benton. The homemade cheeseburgers served there will send you to heaven.

"If they have a jumbo cheeseburger get it! And french fries, too!" were Amanda's last words as I grabbed my car keys.

Upon my arrival, I began scanning over the menu painted on a sign outside. I located a jumbo cheeseburger and fries, then placed my order.

We devoured our jumbo cheeseburgers, made just like Mamma Betty's. Well, not just like hers, but similar. (I want to be careful here because there is a chance of getting some dumplins'.)

I rated this jumbo cheeseburger "three napkins." It

was the kind of burger that when I took a bite, the juice ran down to my elbows. (Mama Betty's was a "four-napkins.")

Sometimes life calls for a good, old-fashioned, homemade cheeseburger. If you're not as fortunate as I am, blessed with a wonderful mama-in-law who can make the best burger you ever sank your teeth into, then let me suggest Loy's Snack Shop in Benton.

One more thing. This place had french fried pickles on the menu. I have never had that delicacy. I suppose we Southerners will eat any type of food that is deep fried. It is an adventure to try something different.

Ah, life's simple pleasures!

Southern Pizza Called 'Bubba'

Hungry for Southern-style pizza? If so, ask for the "Bubba."

A co-worker recommended that if I wanted a good pizza with a ton of stuff piled high on top, I should ask for a "Bubba" served at a local restaurant.

I called a local pizza establishment and asked if they had a "Bubba."

"We have a Bubba who works here," a woman said.

"No. You don't understand. Do you have a 'Bubba' pizza?" I asked.

"Bubba, who works here, is the only Bubba in the place," she said with thunderous laughter. "You wouldn't want him on your pizza, would you?"

I assured her that I didn't want Bubba, or anyone from his immediate family, climbing on top of my pizza.

"I believe I have the wrong number," I finally said.

As I hung up the receiver, sounds of laughter could still be heard.

Another local pizza factory was called.

"Do you have a 'Bubba'?" I asked, praying I had the right place.

"We sure do," a woman said.

"That's great! I'll take a medium 'Bubba'" I said.

"Give us 15 minutes," she said.

This time, I couldn't stop laughing. After I told Amanda about my mixed-up order, she laughed and said, "They probably get a lot of calls like that." There are at least six pizza manufacturing diners in Benton, but only one serves the "Bubba."

I doubt if you will find a pizza named "Bubba" on the East Side of New York City or in the windy city of Chicago, only in the South. Even at that, I doubt that very many restaurants in Arkansas serve a pizza with that name.

Next, we may hear of a Southern-style jumbo cheeseburger called the "Bubba" burger. Eventually, a trip around the all-you-can-eat salad bar might be referred to as the "Bubba" salad. A generous helping of barbecue would be an important item to be included on the salad menu.

A quick look through the pages of a handy dictionary states:

- **bubba** *n.* – 1. A thang that is gigantic, as in, a Goodyear blimp. Example: "Say, that's a *bubba* of a bruise you've got there on your arm." 2. A large Southern man who wears a baseball cap and drives a "Big-foot" pickup truck. Example: "Hey Bubba, crushed any cars lately?"

Naturally, the "Bubba" pizza was big, good and stuck to my ribs. (When a particular food was good and good for you, my mother would say, "It will stick to your ribs.")

I would bet that every Southern man, woman and child knows of or is kin to a "Bubba." A good friend and college roommate of mine was Bubba Smith.

Maybe tonight would be a good time to take your Bubba out for a "Bubba."

The Joy of Chicken Fried Steak

Well, I'm back at the food trough again. This time the highlight is another southern delicacy – chicken-fried steak smothered in cream gravy.

This palatal prize has been known by other names including southern-fried, country-fried and breaded steak.

I'm a bit confused about the name chicken-fried steak. Why do we refer to it as chicken-fried when no part of a chicken is used to prepare this southern dish?

Cherie Ward, Courier lifestyles editor, believes it is "chicken-fried" because you prepare it like fried chicken. Still confused, I sought a second opinion.

I referred my question to Suzanne Brown, Courier food editor, for an authoritative answer. "It is prepared the same way you prepare chicken to fry, " she said. Leave it up to the southern cooks to know.

I love chicken-fried steak. That's what Amanda, Betty Jo (my favorite mamma-in-law), Nathan (my step son) and I ordered recently at Clyde's restaurant on Edison Avenue in Benton. Gramps (my favorite daddy-in-law) ordered a vegetable plate.

When the order arrived, Nathan and I looked at each other and then at our plates. We noticed the chicken-fried steaks ordered by Betty Jo and Amanda were larger than the ones we had in front of us. We felt a bit discriminated against.

Our opinion changed as we began to devour this wonderful example of a southern, home-cooked meal. The chicken-fried steak was thick and juicy, surrounded with just the right texture of batter and smothered with a delightful cream gravy.

It became apparent to Nathan and me that, although Amanda's and Betty Jo's steaks seemed larger, we had more than we needed. However, I probably could have eaten another half of one. It was that delicious.

We are blessed in the south with so many good cooks and such a wide variety of cookbooks. But, a lot of really good cooks have no need to follow a recipe. A pinch of this, a pinch of that, is about all they use. Taste plays a large role in southern cooking.

A diet is difficult to pull off when one is in the midst of so many good cooks and an abundance of great places to break bread with family and friends.

A family that eats together probably needs to diet together.

Cow Patty Trail

What I am about to tell you is no joke. These are actual, verified names of roads, lanes, drives and trails located in Saline County. Some are hilarious bringing laughter and others bringing wonderment.

The first name that caught my attention was Cow Patty Trail located just off Kruse Loop. One could think of a host of variations on that name. Once this name is spoken out loud, a grin will begin at one corner of your mouth and will not stop until it unfolds into a full-fledged smile, perhaps even a chuckle. I learned that three families reside on historic Cow Patty Trail.

The county definitely has a sweet tooth with Candy Cane and M&M lanes.

Old Maid's Road makes a statement about marriage, or lack of it.

We even have the beginning of the day depicted in Dawn Drive and Day Bright Circle.

A favorite style of music can be reached via Dixieland Road.

There must be many good cooks on Kitchen Road. Then there's Bean Road. Dare I say more?

Gourd Neck Road and Lime Kill Holler Road

probably have a local history as to the origin of their names.

The name of creeks within the county is another matter.

Mud Creek was probably not named by the state Pollution Control and Ecology folks.

I could have named Lost Creek. It would have been my misfortune to become disoriented during a camping trip. However, during my adventure, my luck would probably have brought me to Dry Creek.

My bird-hunting buddies probably named Duck Creek. After the first shot, another creek was named Drop Creek.

Environmentalists, making their way down to Duck Creek, could have suggested the name of Chipmunk Road.

Love Creek produces thoughts of summer days and skinny-dipping. I'm not sure of the location, but Pleasure Drive should be near Love Creek.

A southern county would not be complete without a "Ya'll come back now" road. In Saline County we have Friendly Lane.

These are a few of the names that depict life in Saline County. Some folks may call the names foolish. Others may take these names seriously. In any event, the names are real.

I have heard that parents ought to be careful in choosing a name for their new baby because they have to live with it. Could this axiom apply to county roads?

No Mailing Address – Only Map

One of the most enjoyable moments in a person's life can be when a letter is delivered with his or her name on it. There is not a single human being that does not look forward to receiving personal mail. When the morning mail brings a reminder of an unpaid bill, well, that's another story.

Early American history books detail stories of just how dangerous delivering mail was at one time. During those Old West days, it took months or even years for people to receive mail in spite of the noble efforts of the Pony Express.

Today, if mail isn't received within several days, our first thought is: "Well, I guess the horse must have died." (Complaints about postal service date back to the days of the Pony Express.)

A small part of postal history recently traveled across my desk via a photocopy of an old envelope. This particular piece of mail caused me to ponder just how far this country has progressed in terms of mail delivery.

The envelope had been hand-stamped and postmarked "North Hollywood, California, 1:30 p.m., Feb. 4, 1946." The letter required only a 3-cent stamp to assure its safe arrival to the post office at Detonti, Arkansas.

This did not surprise me. What did was the address. The envelope read as follows:

This letter is going to Uncle Lee down in Tull, Arkansas, Grant County, between Mud Creek and Saline River, and across the field from Uncle Hardy's better known as Detonti, Arkansas, RR#1

The return address was:

From his nephew Grady DuVall out in California

The late Milton Sheppard was the rural mail carrier who delivered DuVall's letter. It's a wonder the letter made it through at all, addressed as it was. Truth is, indeed, stranger than fiction.

During those years in California, Grady DuVall frequently sent letters to Uncle Lee and Aunt Mattie Jacobs back home in Tull and they would always arrive at Uncle Lee's place.

The price of postage to mail a letter has only increased 26 cents in 45 years. That's about one-half cent per year.

Although it costs us 26 cents more for postage than it did in 1946, I doubt that many letters addressed like the 1946 model would be deliverable today, even for 29 cents.

My Uncle Harold was employed as a teller in the post office in Texarkana. The stateline, dividing Arkansas from Texas, ran down the middle of the post office building.

As a youngster, I would often climb the many steps

to enter the hallowed halls of this post office. Once in, I would walk over to my uncle's window and ask him to stamp *Air Mail* on top of my hand. He never failed to comply.

I remember when an envelope could be addressed "City" and it would be delivered simply by locating the address in Texarkana. That was before zip codes.

Uncle Harold never cared too much for the new system. Nowadays, not only is a zip code required for mail service, but in some cases, it has doubled in numbers.

To paraphrase Mark Twain, the only thing sent that does not require postage or zip codes is prayer. But give the federal government a few more years and I'm sure they'll find a way.

So Close and Yet So Far Away

One of the most embarrassing moments in a person's life occurs when the car keys are locked up inside the car. I can't recall how many times I have managed to perform this feat. It really doesn't matter. Once is enough.

I was in Bryant, Arkansas, on a photo assignment to take a few pictures at a reception in honor of Dr. Ralph Izard's return from a tour of duty in Operation Desert Storm.

After a few shots were snapped, I made my way to my car. My pockets felt lighter than usual. A sinking feeling began to hit me. Sure enough, I found my keys, safe and sound, locked up inside.

I immediately returned to Dr. Izard's office and asked a nurse for a coat hanger. I didn't have to tell her why I needed it. She knew.

While I was struggling with the coat hanger, a good friend of mine drove up and asked if he could help. Buzz May offered to call the police from his vehicle and check on a "slim jim," a device to open a car door.

Buzz talked with Police Chief James Alvin Hipps and found out the police no longer use this instrument. Soon Hipps arrived on the scene.

By this time, I had forgotten about the crowd

gathered at the reception who, by the way, could see every move of our attempt to open the door.

Marilyn Lee, Bryant postmaster, drifted up to the car on her way to the reception. She told us we could probably buy one of those devices for about $6 across the street at Crazy Cal's. It was good advice, but we decided to continue our operation because of the time already invested.

More time passed.

Stansel Harvey, Saline Memorial Hospital administrator, Greg Rickel, SMH assistant administrator, and two other men whom I assumed were doctors, entered the scene. I can still hear Stansel laughing at my predicament.

"Is there a surgeon in the bunch?" I asked. No response. Buzz continued working with the door, assisted by James Alvin.

James Alvin figured that if we could hook the coat hanger around the small window handle, we could open it enough to get a hand through to pull up the door lock.

Well. It worked.

Buzz reached through the window, but after several attempts, could not quite lift the lock. I saw a light bulb turn on just above Buzz's head. He pulled his arm back and then reached about eight inches to the ignition and retrieved the car keys.

James Alvin gave me a polite lecture on the

importance of having a second set of keys made. I assured him that is exactly what I would do.

I told the crew how grateful I was for their help and promised, again, that I would get another set of keys made.

The saga continues.

An evening assignment took me to a Saline County Quorum Court meeting. I walked out the back door and slammed it shut behind me. That same sinking feeling hit me again.

You guessed it. I locked my keys inside the house. John and Jessica were watching a television program. Amanda was busy in another part of the house. I managed to get John's attention to open the door.

"Dad, you locked your keys inside the house," John said with a laugh. I shrugged the mishap off and drove to my night meeting.

One more incident.

I hadn't read that evening's *Courier* so I stopped at Smith Caldwell Drug Store to pick up a paper. I placed my 35 cents into the slot. I wasn't really surprised when I couldn't get the rack door to open. My money was lost and I didn't get a paper. It was just that kind of day.

Some days are diamonds and others are stone, wrote singer/songwriter John Denver. This day was definitely a boulder.

Days are just that – days. They are neither good nor

bad. Perhaps it's not the day being terrible so much as it's where a person's thoughts are during the day. Mine were a million miles away.

So, I guess it's up to us. We determine what kind of day we'll have. Tomorrow will be better. Thank God this day is over.

Have a good one, tomorrow!

Southern Pickup Trucks

You can't write a country song without the mention of mothers, prisons, trains, guns, whiskey, broken hearts or pickup trucks.

I remember the simple pleasure of riding in the back of a pickup. On a summer day, it's you and the dog and the wind blowing through your hair. I can't remember whose truck it was. However, I do recall horses, cows, and a distinct odor associated with the ride.

The pickup truck has long remained an American symbol. In some circles, people have considered this unique vehicle to be the "Cowboy's Cadillac." Today, trucks are bought by business executives, housewives and yuppies. They are not just for cowboys and cowgirls anymore.

Southern trucks, to be regarded as what some think are real trucks, must have a certain decor about them. Among the special designer items is a gun rack mounted in the cab. Usually, one or two rifles drape the rack, although I have seen fishing rods nestled in some.

Another important feature is an eye-catching bumper sticker. Some of the messages include such variations as: **Caution while Passing - Driver is Chewing Tobacco; If Guns were Outlawed, only Outlaws**

would have Guns; God, Guns and Guts made America; Let's Keep it that Way; American Ends with I CAN; not IRAN and the ever-popular **I (heart) My Truck.**

One more accessory that may complete a Southern truck's ensemble is a Confederate flag hanging in the back window.

Truck owners have a profound attitude about their vehicles. I guess the problem is not so much attitude, but altitude. Some trucks apparently can climb over multileveled buildings. They have enormous tires that raise them up so high off the ground that you need an elevator to get behind the steering wheel. After you make the climb, oxygen tanks might be necessary.

You never know how many friends you have until you buy a pickup truck. It doesn't have to be "Big Foot" to get attention. Just a standard Ford, Chevrolet or Dodge will do. (I don't consider little Japanese truckettes as real trucks.)

When you need a truck, you **REALLY** need a truck. The back seat of the car will not get it. For example, you've recently bought a house after living in an apartment. In two days everything must be moved out. Parked on the street in front of your house is a 1968 Volkswagen Beetle – not big enough for the great exodus.

Nerves become frayed, sweat beads pop up on your forehead and you scream, "I need a truck!" In desperation, you turn to your wife and ask if she knows of anyone who has a truck.

She returns home from work the next day with an announcement. "There is a guy at work, who has a friend, who has a friend that has a truck," she says. "We can borrow it Thursday."

My father-in-law, James "Cap" Adams, has a couple of trucks. One is a diesel and the other is . . . well, it's a truck. Amanda and I affectionately call it "Old Green." You can see the ground through the hole in the floor board. If the brakes hang up and stick, Cap says, "Just get out and kick the fool out of the tire."

We are grateful for the use of "Old Green" for a number of reasons. We've used it on many trips to the dump and for moving an assortment of stuff.

During my high school years, I noticed that if a clean-cut, short-haired boy in a pickup truck drove into a girl's driveway to take her out on a date, her parents didn't say too much. However, if a long-haired boy driving a van came by to take her out, questions spewed forth like Old Faithful. I never quite figured that one out.

One of these days, I'm going to purchase a pickup truck. Until then, I'll simply rely on the graciousness of Cap, Paul Sawyer and other truckers.

Isn't it great to own one of these American-made southern symbols?

Life Goes On

No matter if tragedies have struck, or illnesses have us bound, or heartaches cause us pain, or joys and celebrations are in the air . . . life does goes on .

Life's Full of Little Frustrations

Some things are difficult to open, while others are downright difficult to get into – like cars on rainy days and the stubborn wrappers on some candy bars.

I get angry, frustrated and wet as I try to gracefully enter my car on a rainy day. Once in the seat, my next strategic maneuver centers around how to get my umbrella inside without getting drenched.

Surrounded by wind and rain, I attempt to keep the car door open with my left foot and pull down the umbrella until it locks. My clothes are soaked as I finally close the umbrella. Whew! Now the rain drips on me again as I search for the appropriate place in my car for a wet umbrella.

I really do love rainy days, but I think they are best enjoyed by staying in bed and watching the moisture drip from the window ledge.

Recently, frustrations accumulated as I tried to get into a white chocolate candy bar. When I took the outer wrapper off, the bar was hermetically sealed with a non-biodegradable-petroleum-based-plastic-aluminum type paper. Printed on one end were these words – *tear here* – accompanied by little arrows that traveled around the end.

I followed the instructions, but I was unable to open

the candy bar. Upon further investigation, I noticed a second set of words and arrows on the opposite end. "I must really be hungry to get this involved," I told myself.

One end finally opened, but I still couldn't get the bar out. I ate the candy piece by piece, literally digging it out of the wrapper. What an ordeal for a sweet tooth!

In her wisdom, Amanda pointed out that both ends are supposed to be opened. (She had previously gone through this particular process.) "That is why they have it written on both ends," she said.

Why are so many things difficult to get into these days?

If a person dreams of being elected to a political office, he or she must raise an enormous amount of money just to enter the race for a position that pays less than what it costs to maintain an adequate campaign. This particular political formula doesn't add up. But, hey, much of the government's spending today makes about as much sense. Enough money can get you into almost any place, even into trouble.

I miss the candy bar wrapped in paper without instructions. Life and candy bars shouldn't be so difficult to get into.

Phrases like "I can't get into that!" are used when someone doesn't want to be involved. However, there are some things we need to get into if we're going to have a future:

    * Keeping our cities and country clean.

    * Supporting our law enforcement agencies' efforts in the war against drugs.

    * Working for cooperation among our neighbors and local government for a better community and discovering ways to help victims of crimes.

These are only a few suggestions. You may have your own issues of importance.

Rain, umbrellas or candy bars are only minor frustrations. It's the major ones that should get on our nerves.

Woman Had Too Much 'Scents'

When is the appropriate time to begin using deodorants, cologne and perfume? How did we ever make it through our "coming of age" years without them? Or have we?

After a day of romping together, a sweaty 6-year-old and a puppy carry a distinct similarity to each other as far as aroma is concerned.

How do you break the news to a young person that it is time to use a roll-on, spray or stick deodorant?

The solution may be to put a bottle of cologne and a spray can of deodorant in their Christmas stocking and wait for a response.

Being interested in the opposite sex usually takes care of a "stinky" situation. Although, I have seen deodorant and cologne designed for elementary school-aged children on department store shelves.

A "scent" problem has always existed. "She smells like a French whore," is a remark made about a woman who wears too much perfume. How much cologne or perfume should be splashed upon a person's body?

With the advent of each new fragrance, we are bombarded by people who seem to have bathed in it.

At a James Taylor concert in Fayetteville, Amanda and I were victims of a woman who obviously took a swim in Estee Lauder.

The woman sent a new wave of perfumed air with every movement. Amanda's sinuses were having a fit and my eyes began to water.

"Can't this woman smell herself?" I thought.

She left her seat several times during the concert. I believe she added a few more drops of perfume while in the powder room.

Perhaps all this perfume and cologne splashing has something to do with the price of the stuff. "If I pay $50 for 2 ounces, I want people to smell how much I spent," one person might say.

In my early years, the choices for men's cologne were simple. The fragrances included Old Spice, English Leather, Brut, and British Sterling. For a brief moment, an Arkansas man could purchase a bottle of Hog Sweat. (I think the name had an adverse affect on sales.)

People in offices often mention people's perfumes. Sometimes the only good thing said about a person was that he or she smelled good.

The only deodorants available in my younger years seemed to be Right Guard and Ban. We sprayed. We splashed. We had little regard for the damage being done to the ozone level. Now we combat this awareness with a host of non-aerosol sprays.

Cleanliness is next to godliness, but too much scents is next to impossible.

The next time we apply cologne or perfume to our bodies, remember others. It is not always a good thing to be considered "breathtaking."

Pondering Life in a Treehouse

I must have slept through it, because I did not hear the sounds of a recent thunderstorm. The next morning, I discovered the storm's evidence scattered in my yard. High winds apparently blew a tree limb into our neighbor's yard. Amanda and I discovered a nearly-severed limb under the direction of the neighbor.

There it was, bigger than Dallas, laying across her clothesline. She didn't ask me or Amanda to climb the tree, cut off the limb and pull it into our yard. We thought it was the neighborly thing to do.

This particular chore was not on our "Top 10 Things to Do" list on that Sunday morning. Our list included cleaning out the garage; not climbing a tree.

I made the climb through rain-soaked leaves and tree limbs. (Being sprinkled by water from wet leaves can almost ruin a morning.) I began to saw away as Amanda guided the broken limbs so that no damage would be done to fences, shrubs and other items around the tree.

While I was in the tree, I cut not only that limb, but several others that draped over the fence along the row in the backyard. I really didn't mind it that much. We have plans to build a wooden fence around the backyard. The choice: cut them now or cut them later.

I couldn't remember the last time I had climbed a tree. While cradled in its large branches, I wondered why I haven't climbed more often? The answer came to me gradually, along with aches and pains and the realization that the old body is not as flexible as it once was.

Once I nestled in, I thought, "this would be a perfect place for a tree house." It was not too high, but high enough to look over the house.

When I was a little whippersnapper, I constructed a tree house in a wild cherry tree in my backyard. It served as a clubhouse.

With the help of a rope, my buddies and I pulled up all the essentials into our clubhouse. These rations included peanut butter and jelly sandwiches, a thermos of Kool-Aid and a few comic books for an afternoon of reading.

We had gotten a lot of our good ideas from viewing the movie *Swiss Family Robinson* shown at the Strand Theatre in downtown Texarkana.

I loved to climb that tree when I was younger. I would make my way up into the branches on Friday nights and listen to the play-by-play being given over the loud speakers at Buhrman Field. I would root for the home football team from my lofty perch.

Another form of excitement provided me by my tree house was the ability to watch cars and trucks pass underneath me on 24th Street. (This was the main drag for local teenagers).

The wild cherry tree is now a stump.

Now, I find comfort and enjoyment in sitting on my front porch and watching cars glide down Cross Street in Benton.

Until this latest episode with the broken tree limbs, it had been a long time since I had climbed a tree.

I would like to say climbing trees was a barrel of fun. I would like to – but I can't. Perhaps the task might have been a little more enjoyable 25 years ago.

While in that tree, I had a few brief moments to think about life while I gave my arm a rest from sawing. Maybe it would be helpful if everyone had their own tree to climb and a little time devoted just to sit and think.

We all need a place to ponder.

Letter Becomes an Inspiration

I discovered something of myself and it wasn't even lost – only covered up. It was hidden among such things as old picture frames, outdated magazines and a fine collection of plaster of Paris molds.

My mother saves everything from aluminum pie pans to every hat she has ever purchased. (She believes hats are never out of style.) Most of us save coupons, newspaper articles, an assortment of catalogues and old letters.

During a visit with my parents, my father found a box of old cards sent to them when I was born. Why save all of these? Only a mother can answer that one. As my father began to read some of them out loud, my ears caught the words of one card in particular. It was written by a cousin of the family, Lorraine Conner, who resides in Dallas.

The letter, dated Nov. 10, 1952, reads, in part, as follows:

Dear Little Haley,
Welcome to this old world!

I am sorry it is so troubled, but maybe you, or someone you shall know, is the one destined to set it right.

I earnestly hope that you included in your bundle of possessions, when you packed up to come among us, a

goodly lot of talents, whether music, song or art, for this
old world needs all the beauty it can get.

And when you have reached your teens may your
personality and manners be so charming that all will wel -
come you who knows you.

Thus you will reach Man's Estate with all the en -
dowments of leadership.

You start by being a good little boy, minding Mother
and Father, then teacher, then your own Conscience will
take over.

May your life be personally very happy.

Tears welled up in my eyes as I read the yellowed
fragment from my wonderful reception into this world.
However, I wish I could have read the letter before almost
four decades had passed. Perhaps, I would have heeded its
timely wisdom.

It is a tragic flaw in human nature that wisdom from
the older sages is wasted on the young. However, most of
life can only be experienced; not taught. We simply agree
with wisdom after we have been through our own trials,
tribulations, pains and heartaches.

I will take these words to heart and try to pass them
on to others in some way. Thank you, cousin. Hopefully
some of your words found their way into my lifestyle.

We may call them "guardian angels." They are the
people who have been in our corner from the first day our

tiny nostrils took a deep breath of life. They are silent partners in our upbringing and over the years, have been aware
of our ups and downs and have kept us in their prayers.

I have never met this cousin. She taught many years
in Dallas' Highland Park School. Maybe she believed her
guiding words might encourage me in the years ahead.

Each one of us has the potential to make a difference
in the way this old world turns on its axis. You may be the
one who encourages the Nobel Prize winner for the year
2000.

I agree with my cousin, this planet could stand a bit
more beauty. It has enough garbage.

The Broken Mirror Blues

It is amazing to me that out of all the days of the year, one day can gain control over most human beings. The day is Friday the 13th. Some people circle that date on their calendars and take a day of vacation. Others are alarmed to discover the day just crept up on them. Or did it?

I have no idea how the number 13 and the day of Friday produced so much bad luck when mixed together. There are folks who are very superstitious. You might even be a bit superstitious when it comes to certain things.

Everybody knows that it is bad luck to allow a black cat to cross your path. Some cross the street on the other side if they believe this is about to take place, or, simply turn around and walk in the opposite direction.

Henry Hunt, a retired men's clothing salesman with Belk-Jones in Texarkana, was (and probably still is) superstitious in regard to black cats.

On several occasions, Mr. Hunt has been spotted doing odd things while driving his car. He has lifted his hat off his head, turned it around and returned it back to his head. Why? Because a black cat had just crossed the street in front of him.

I guess he thought it would be permissible to at least turn his hat around instead of making a u-turn in the middle of County Avenue. I wonder what kind of luck he had had by making this type of gesture?

I remember a particular Friday the 13th. I was sent home from high school and ordered to get a haircut. My hair barely touched the top of my ears and the top of my shirt collar. I was not in the best of moods.

During the course of the day, I managed to run a red light, receive a speeding ticket, break a mirror and get a haircut. I really believe it had something to do with getting a haircut. What kind of mood are you in when you get a haircut and it's too short? Well, that's my point.

One Friday the 13th recently caught me off guard. I completely forgot about its significance. Amanda apparently did as well. When it dawned on her that this was bad luck day she said, "Do you know what I did today? I broke our hand mirror." Just what we need, I thought. What is it now, seven years of bad luck and give up our first born male child? Well, we will take our chances.

I believe what we do not understand, we attribute to either good or bad luck. We travel through life equipped with our little idiosyncrasies and habits and often throw caution to the wind.

A line from the song *Born Under a Bad Sign* seems to sum up some thoughts on the subject: If it weren't for bad luck, I wouldn't have any luck at all.

Some people appear to be lucky. Everything they

touch turns to gold. For most of us, everything we touch turns to something else.

We are creatures of habit and live either by fate or faith or both.

As soon as I find my rabbit's foot I will be in good shape.

Moo Juice in Moderation

In my opinion, just about everything goes well with a tall, cold glass of milk. I love "moo juice," especially with a plate of homemade peanut butter cookies, several pieces of pecan pie, or a couple of slices of Amanda's strawberry cake. From the first time my tastebuds were tantalized by milk, I've been addicted to it. I drank so much milk as a youngster that my parents considered buying a cow.

The plan was to dangle the cow's udders through the kitchen window and save on the daily purchase of a gallon of milk. It would be handy. Open the window and grab an udder. What a marvelous innovation. Little doubt that our family would have been the first on our block to have such a milk dispenser.

In the days when my father (now 78) was attending elementary school, he was considered thin. My guess is the teachers got together and thought he needed fattening up a bit. The solution: give Kenneth Haley more milk and plenty of it. Well, it must have started a chain reaction because he hasn't stopped eating since that time.

He tells the story of how he was fired from his job as a soda jerk at a drugstore in Clarksville, Tennessee, because he would make milkshakes, hot fudge sundaes, or banana splits for himself when there was a slack time in business. Soon his stomach bulged, his pockets stuck out and the boss noticed where most of the "would-be profits" were going. My father left soon after that.

My dad recalls a day he walked past a large mirror in front of a store after he had inhaled about three hamburgers and a hot dog. (I may be off a little on the menu, but not by much.) He stopped, looked into the mirror and noticed the figure of a fat man. Several candy bars were sticking out of his pants pocket. He was stunned.

Dad was soon drafted into the Army, not to lose weight, but to serve his country. He entered weighing near the 300-pound mark.

Most soldiers dreaded KP duty, but not my father. He told me stories of how banana pudding (one of his all time favorites) would come to the camp in large barrels. With a large spoon in hand, my dad would clean out the pudding that remained in the "empties."

The scales tipped at about 198 pounds when he received his honorable discharge from the service.

In past years, I have seen my father sit down with a half gallon of vanilla ice cream, eat out the center, add a sliced banana and drip chocolate syrup on top, and finish it in one setting.

I think his weight problem began years ago when the extra cartons of milk were used to correct his thinness.

However, I don't want milk to take all the blame for my father's enjoyment of food.

Reports have indicated that milk is not that good for people my age or older, at least not in the amount I consume. It seems to me that just about everything we like carries some flaw with it. Sometimes, I want to eat and drink anything I have a taste for regardless of the proposed long-term side effects.

I have never heard a bad word said about oysters. Those slimy globs of goo are disgusting to me. However, research hasn't determined that there are any aftereffects of this seafood delight. So, I guess they aren't that terrible. (My father can eat his weight in them.)

Oh well, maybe the appropriate word here is moderation, no matter what it is.

Frustrations at a Drive-In Bank

Waiting in long lines at a drive-in bank can be a frustrating experience. Sometimes I wonder what's going through a person's mind the moment after they take the canister, place their deposit slip and payroll check inside and press the "send" button.

We receive our checks at about 10:30 a.m. on Fridays. Some of us immediately sign out and rush to deposit them. At this time of day, long lines have started to form at the drive-in window. Trying to find the shortest line reminds me of playing "rush-in roulette."

On one particular day, I was lucky enough to pull into the shortest line. In front of me was a woman who apparently left home too early to make out her deposit slip. When she began to brush her hair, I knew I was going to be in line for quite some time. By now I was trapped. I couldn't switch lines. I just thought I was lucky.

After she brushed her hair, she began putting on her makeup. I started to squirm when I realized the woman knew she had time to primp.

"If she begins to change her clothes in the car, I'm outta here!" I said to myself.

I'm getting fidgety now.

The other lines of cars were slowly thinning out. As I looked around, I realized I was the only one left in line except for this woman.

As she drove away, I noticed a sticker in her back window made in the image of a California license plate bearing the words: NEARLY NORMAL. I had no more questions.

I struck up a conversation with Jan Spivey, one of the drive-in tellers, in regard to some of the reasons why the lines move so slowly.

Jan, a delightful person with a great sense of humor, said some folks are unprepared before making a deposit. There are others who can't remember their bank account number. Some have forgotten their pens after they realized their deposit slip was not filled out, while others have never learned how to fill one out at all.

I told her I couldn't understand why people aren't prepared. They must know ahead of time about their trip to make a deposit. Jan agreed. I had said to her in a previous visit that I would write a column on the frustrations of drive-in bank tellers and dealing with absent-minded depositors.

The other day I was in line to make my deposit when it happened; I forgot to write my savings account number on my deposit slip.

"Do you know your number?" Jan asked with a grin.

I told her I didn't. She assured me she could find it out quickly. Well, at this moment, I'm embarrassed knowing the people behind me are wondering why I didn't fill out my deposit slip before I came.

"You're one of them now," Jan said with a laugh.

"Now I'll have to write about me," I told her.

Before I could drive off, Jan called back and said she had forgotten to include my receipt. I sent the canister back. She included my receipt and returned the canister. I opened it, shook out the receipt, and hurried away.

Moments later at *The Benton Courier* parking lot, I realized my checkbook and my money were gone.

I quickly phoned Jan about my dilemma. She said an older lady found it in the canister and turned it in. Thank God (and the senior citizen).

Jan was right. I'm one of "them" now.

How about you? Are you one of "them" as well? It appears that you and I are NEARLY NORMAL.

It Was On Sale

"Well, it was on sale." This was just one of the comments overheard at a close-out sale at a local department store. Sales are an American tradition.

"I just came in here to buy an outdoor extension cord," one package burdened woman said. "I spent $58, but I saved $24."

"You know, Margaret has a birthday coming up," a lady said to her weary husband as she stood staring at birthday cards.

We have the passionate desire to buy presents for everybody when there's a sale going on. It takes great restraint and will power to pass up a sale. Most of us want something for nothing and we often end up with just that – nothing. We buy clothes that almost fit and we purchase colors we've never worn before in our lives.

My father cannot pass up something on sale. One day he brought home 15 bags of toasted, coconut covered marshmallows after a romp down the sale aisle of a department store.

There is something intoxicating about the word SALE. The very sound entices us to come a bit closer, luring us like a carnival barker at a county fair. Isn't it amazing

what happens when a few adjectives are placed before the
word sale.

*Going-out-of-business, final reduction, hail
damage, smoke damage, over-stocked, quitting business,
close-out, liquidation, sidewalk, half-price, everything-
must-go, pre-inventory and the 50% off* sales are some
good examples.

We keep our religious and national heritage alive, as
well as educate our children, with holiday sales such as
Washington's Birthday, Memorial Day, the Fourth of July,
President's Day, Lincoln's Birthday, Thanksgiving Day,
Easter, After-Easter, Pre-Christmas, Christmas, After-
Christmas and Labor Day.

I'll bet you a dollar to a bagel that stacked in a closet
somewhere, you have a remnant of a sale gone by. You just
couldn't pass it up. It was on sale.

These bargains are passed on to neighbors, enemies,
in-laws and total strangers through that famous event that
takes place on any given weekend of the year – garage sales.

There are folks who never pay full price for
anything. It doesn't matter to them that perhaps the lapels on
a sportscoat are a bit too wide, or that a tie is large enough to
protect a clean shirt from accidental food spills.

Some folks have sales shopping down to a fine art.
They cannot understand why anyone buys merchandise at
full price. These people want others to know how much they

paid for an item on sale, but they are a bit reluctant to divulge any numbers if they paid the full price.

I enjoy a sale as much as anyone. My adventurous spirit soars as I fight the multitude of customers. My athletic ability is challenged as I duck the grabbing hands reaching for the sweaters. I'm polite at first, then it's no more Mr. Nice Guy. It's everyone for himself. Coming back home with the booty like a conquering hero, I sit back and beam with pride as I read my receipt.

Go ahead and buy something just because it is on sale. You will feel better. Besides, you deserve it.

Laughter is Healing

If laughter is the best medicine, why aren't more doctors prescribing it?

Reading the doctor's prescription can be difficult. However, when it comes to deciphering the amount of the bill, it's crystal clear. That's no laughing matter. We need to laugh when we get the bill to keep from crying.

I come from a line of Haleys who are practical jokers and storytellers. My father is a funny man.

However, when you have known him as long as I have, you have heard most of the jokes at least three times.

I've numbered and cataloged all his jokes. We sit around and shout B-25 and laugh, followed by hearty chuckles at the mention of T-245. Have you heard R-78? You'll laugh until your sides are splitting. I believe it has something to do with working as a salesman for Sherwin Williams paint store for 35 years. The outside salesmen always had a few new jokes. Since his retirement, he doesn't get a new batch.

Laughter is good medicine. Norman Cousins, the author and playwright, was diagnosed as having an incurable disease. Hospitalized, Cousins had an assortment of movies like The Keystone Cops, Charles Chaplin, The

Three Stooges and other slapstick comedians sent to his
room.

Merriment burst throughout his hospital room. The
deep, belly laughs helped Cousins regain his strength and
eventually his health.

Many medical reports have stated that when a person
laughs, a chemical is released within the body that seems to
be a healing agent. Humor is also heralded as a healing agent
in relationships, including marriages.

If we can take ourselves less seriously, inject some
laughter, and see the funny side of life, we can make it
through difficult times more easily.

I believe laughter is a gift from God. It is a
marvelous blessing to us. We need to call it forth in our
lives. When God made the platypus (a beaver with a duck-
bill) out of spare parts, I bet he had a good chuckle. When
God made the avocado seed too large, His eternal grin
probably stretched across the heavens. When Sarah was
scheduled to have a baby about the time she was to pick up
her Social Security check, God, Sarah and Abraham all
laughed and they named the baby Isaac (which means
laughter).

I'm certain God was only joking when He put the
idea of making "leisure suits" into the mind of a New York
designer.

Comedy clubs have emerged across our country.

They are in large cities and small towns. People stand in line for a laugh. For a few hours, people are healed by laughter and manage to forget their problems.

Life can be very difficult for us at times. On occasions we feel we are at the end of our rope. During those trying moments, all we have is a laugh. But it is good to laugh. Tomorrow is another day. We need to laugh more.

When God made you and me, a spark of laughter was planted in our hearts. Cultivating its power is up to us. Did you hear the one about the . . . well maybe you have. I see you smiling.

That's great.

Heroes Are Everyday People

Where are all our heroes?

Who qualifies as a hero? Mr. Webster defines a hero as: Any person admired for qualities or achievements and regarded as an ideal or model.

I would say a hero is one who inspires and does not act as a role model. Role models have clay feet and are easily bruised.

All of us have our heroes. Someone we can admire, someone to guide us, or someone who can inspire us.

I don't want to talk about the larger-than-life heroes. We once saw them on the silver screen at Saturday matinees. They leave when popularity goes out the back door.

My heroes are everyday people. They are folks who have faced obstacles in their life and emerged victors.

Beethoven became deaf, but he heard the music in his mind and shared it with the world.

Abraham Lincoln became one of the more gifted presidents of the United States despite enduring more heartaches than Carter's got liver pills.

Franklin D. Roosevelt, stricken with polio, continued to be a strong president through determination.

Mark Twain, a bankrupt dreamer and writer, still

speaks to us through his stories and observations of life.

I want to point out a few unsung heroes:

* The service station owner who loves his work. His smile and courtesy are contagious. The customer trusts him and feels his caring. He is there when you need him.

* The willing church worker who is not stagnated by religious politics, but ventures into areas where no minister has gone (or dares to go).

* The one who doesn't say, " We've never done it this way before."

* The person who is considered a hero, but rarely sees himself as one.

We all have been influenced by relatives, teachers, merchants or other local people. We listened to their stories and were inspired to walk taller, reach higher and really believe in ourselves.

Have you ever considered yourself a hero? Don't laugh. There are some little eyes looking at every move you make. Tiny feet are trying to wear your shoes. Those adorable ears are listening to your every word.

You may be inspiring others simply by overcoming your own difficult situation. Your continued growth in character through adversity may be the example someone gains strength from. You may be an unsung hero to someone simply because you choose to march to a different drummer in a Xerox-copied world.

Heroes dare to be different. They are one of a kind.

Growing Older with Laughter

I learn something about myself each time I travel to my hometown of Texarkana. On a recent trip, my kids and I visited with their grandparents. This time we were on a mission of mercy.

Amanda had worked 56 hours for the week at Little Rock's AT&T plant. In addition, she had also clocked in for Saturday duty. She needed a little peace and quiet. So, off we went to provide her the opportunity for some much needed rest and relaxation.

Soon after I pulled into my parents' driveway, I caught a glimpse of what senior adulthood had in store for me. My parents wanted to take a short trip to Hillcrest Cemetery. The purpose was to view the new family plot marker.

The tombstone had two names etched on the front: WRIGHT-HALEY. My parents and I commented about the craftsmanship of the letters in stone. It was impressive but simple. We all agreed that some shrubbery was needed on either side to balance out the marker.

"Most of the people I know are either in the nursing home or the cemetery," my Dad said as we were standing among some of them. There is a lot of truth to that statement when one reaches a certain age.

Dad and I have a running joke about him and the nursing home. If he does anything out of the ordinary, I might say something like, "That's just like it will be at the Home."

I, like most of you, have said at one point in my life that "I will not be like my parents." But, at times, I sound like both of them. I have also noticed some friends showing traits of their parents.

My future conversations may include one or more of the following:

Organ recitals: A dissertation on the performance of the body parts (heart, eyes, brains, liver, colon) that gives one aches and pains. The body is not like it used to be.

Food prices: The current price of flour, sugar and other food stuffs seem to be a prominent conversation starter. At times our lives revolve around eating.

Weather reports: "Did you get any rain today? It sure is a hot one." Weather conditions can determine what we do in our lives.

* *Observing human behavior*: Comments can be overheard about how old a person looks even though we are the same age.

Obituary readers: Someone dies and we remember seeing them just the other day and they looked good. "I wonder what happened?"

We are all going to be older adults. It will not be by choice. The aging process cannot be stopped. However, on the brighter side, I am looking forward to the many discounts offered to senior adults.

One day I hope to attach a humorous bumpersticker on my RV like many seniors have done. It reads: I'M SPENDING MY CHILDREN'S INHERITANCE.

No matter what our age, I believe we need to cultivate three important words into our living – humor, humor and humor.

With two kids playing and hours of parental conversations during that weekend, I quickly realized how much I love peace and quiet. I was glad to join Amanda in a little "R and R" by Sunday afternoon.

Does life really begin at 40? I'll let you know soon.

Cardboard Hero Investments

I love baseball and have had my share of small town glory. When I played Little League, I pitched a no-hitter and contributed a homerun in the same game.

After I heard my former Pony League coach say I could have become a pro at 16, I tried out with the Texas Rangers in Fort Worth, at the age of 23. Why did he wait so long to tell me?

The only major league baseball game I ever attended was between the L.A. Dodgers and the St. Louis Cardinals in St. Louis. Just before the game started, a dream came true. I watched as Sandy Koufax and Don Drysdale stepped off the team bus. They were bigger than life to this 11-year-old fan.

We all had our baseball heroes. Mays, Mantle, Maris, Drysdale and Koufax, just to mention a few, were mine. All embossed on trading cards.

"I'll trade you Willie Mays for Mickey Mantle," I would say as an 11-year-old, high rolling, baseball-card trader.

Times have changed. Now I'm a baseball card investor. Mantle cards are valued from $300, Mays is just behind Mantle, and Koufax cards are fast approaching the high-price arena.

Wall Street investors have stated in several periodicals that baseball cards rank among gold and silver as investments.

While I was serving as minister in Pine Bluff, Arkansas, in 1981, an 11-year-old parishioner and baseball card entrepreneur asked me, "Brother Tom, do you have any baseball cards?" I assured him that I did and would bring them back the next time I visited my parents in Texarkana.

Shawn and I spread out on his living room floor with a shoebox full of cards and checked them with a price list book. Approximately 60 cards in my collection were valued at a total of about $600. Suddenly, I was really interested in baseball cards. These cards have now doubled in value.

Once I knew Mickey's and Willie's batting average and other vital statistics, but now all I know is their card's market value.

Pain and emptiness engulf me when I think of all the valuable baseball cards I clamped to my bicycle spokes with clothes pins transforming a Schwinn bicycle into a Harley-Davidson motorcycle.

Baseball cards weren't that important to me back in 1961. Besides, the hard sticks of bubblegum accompanying each pack tasted like cardboard. It is a crying shame we only take care of things that seem valuable to us at the time.

My cards are now treated with respect. I have placed each one in a plastic sleeve to protect them from wear and tear.

Mistakes are rewarding when it comes to baseball cards. If the wrong player is pictured on another's card, or if a baseball glove is on the wrong hand, it can make the card even more valuable. A player could be more valuable on a misprinted card than he ever was during his playing career.

Would you trade a Mickey Mantle card for Joe Pepitone?

You're right. I wouldn't either.

Interruptions Can Be Lessons

I hate interruptions with a passion.

I don't know if it's Murphy's Law, but it seems that when the weather report calls for rain, I'm in the middle of my parade.

I guess I'm like most people when I hear the familiar television announcement, **"We interrupt our regularly scheduled program."** I really get irritated.

However, time and experience have taught me patience is better than flying off the handle.

One night the weather report called for a tornado watch. The wind blew fiercely, the sky dropped golf-ball sized hail and the city's weather sirens were bellowing.

Immediately, or close to immediately, Amanda and I grabbed our pillows and jumped into the closet. The scene reminded me of a large bear hugging his wife and settling in for a long winter hibernation.

We are a very happy couple, but something happened in those brief, but tense, moments. The threat of dancing with a tornado created a remarkable opportunity to tell each other a few important things. We shared how much we love each other, our commitment to each other and this deep-rooted love which continues to blossom.

Why all this? You never know what a tornado will do. We could be swept away at any second. This interruption by Mother Nature gave us both a chance to reclaim the essential "stuff" in life that really matters.

The sirens stopped. We emerged from our closet, turned on the television set and began watching a movie. Well, maybe I watched more than Amanda. I was getting interested in the story when suddenly, the piercing sound of a siren began once more.

It was back into the closet with the pillows again. I was watching the movie from the closet when the weatherman interrrupted and told us all about the storm in our area. In my opinion, the television station could have run the weather advisory conditions along the bottom of the screen. I didn't need to see the weatherman's face.

After the report, the movie returned, but the story had progressed so far that I missed some important parts. The station could have stopped the movie, do the report and start the movie where it left off. That would be too good to be true.

Interruptions come to all of us in a variety of ways.

In addition to weather advisories in the middle of televised programs, we have arguments with family and friends, separation and divorce, deaths of loved ones, job disappointments, illnesses and injuries. All are part of life's interruptions.

Perhaps these events are really opportunities to reevaluate our lives and put our priorities in order. We have a chance once again to start over on the right track by answering a few questions for ourselves.

What really matters in life? What gives meaning to our lives? If all our material possessions were taken away, what would we have left?

Amanda and I survived the storm and the sirens. We can always rent the movie we missed. We learned what matters to us.

Maybe life's interruptions can be life's opportunities.

Is it safe to come out of the closet?

Heaven Is a Home

A great exodus begins each summer for many Methodist ministers and their families. The move is the result of several pulpit changes across the states.

Some of you will see them on our interstates and highways. These changes produce two types of rental-truck drivers. One driver will wear a halo and a mile-wide grin singing, "I'll Fly Away" at the top of his lungs and thinking, "I've got it made, the BMW is on the way."

The other will be wearing a red bandana around his forehead while sporting a go-to-hell look and singing 40 renditions of "Take This Job and Shove It." Between verses he will be thinking, "I can't believe this is it, the Bishop's cabinet are a bunch of twits." These nomads of the holy cloth are direct descendants of the children of Israel. They have nowhere to call home. Moving can be a real pain in the southern region of the anatomy. I have my own concept of hell. Here it is:

The story begins as you receive a moving notice after living in a New York home for 15 years with adequate time to accumulate all kinds of "stuff". Many long hours are spent packing and discarding unwanted items. Don't forget the vacated house must be spotlessly clean.

The pain of good-byes and the promises of keeping in touch dance around in your mind, but they begin to fade as you pull away in your truck. Your destination is sunny California. (Hell has nothing to do with California – only the traveling.)

Waiting for you is the perfect house. A spacious lot, sauna and whirlpool are just a few of the luxury items just waiting to be enjoyed.

Your truck almost dies as you approach the driveway. There's no time to rest. Unloading boxes that are stacked a mile high, arranging early attic furniture, feeding your beloved animals and satisfying screaming children are all on your agenda, but your heart is just not into it.

Everything has been unloaded and carefully placed after several knock-down-drag-out fights. There is no rest for the weary. You begin the ritual again.

Searching for boxes at the local liquor stores, packing, trying to rent a truck, and attempting to stay sane through the whole ordeal is just too much to ask.

You guessed it. It's back to New York. This merry-go-round continues for eternity. That's hell to me.

This brings me to my point. Amanda and I recently moved. This move was heaven. We bought a house and left a nice – but small – one bedroom apartment. We also said good-bye to some of the friendliest landlords and neighbors in town.

We are excited. Our house is only three blocks away from *The Benton Courier*.

Four hours a week will be saved by having our own washer and dryer. We no longer have to lug rolls of quarters to be deposited in the laundromat machines. However, I do miss all the regular characters there . . . well, maybe not that much.

Owning a home is a first for me. In my years as a nomad minister, I never had an opportunity to have one. It was always a parsonage, fully equipped with a parsonage committee.

Thank God this move was different. There was no parsonage committee waiting to help us unload. No anxious church members wondering what kind of creatures we were. No plastic smiles or sweaty handshakes. No preconceived notions or impressions.

We were greeted by a house that needed cleaning, painting and an overall face-lifting. That was okay with Amanda and me. It is our home and we have dreams and plans for it.

Whether you live in a small apartment or spacious mansion, home is where the heart is.

How's your heart and home?

Patience Aids a Stress-Free Job

When I was a young boy, I loved to put model airplanes and cars together. It never seemed to fail that after the model was completed, several parts remained in the box screaming to be added.

I don't know if this was caused by my thoughts moving a bit faster than my hands, impatience or simply boredom with instructions. Whatever the reason, it haunts me to this day.

Boxes which carry words like "some assembly required" or "only a screwdriver is needed for assembly" usually include a full sheet of instructions. These instructions are written in at least two languages, possibly three: English, Spanish and Korean. I have trouble following instructions written in English.

Often, I spend more time reassembling a product than actually putting it together. There is a method to this madness.

Amanda has the patience of Job. The first thing she does is read the instructions. Then she locates all the tools necessary for the job, separates the parts and refers back to the instruction sheet. It's a step by step process which produces less frustration and tension. I am learning to take time to read instructions more closely now.

There are several of us in this society that never read instruction manuals. We blindly leap into a project only to discover midway through the course that we need a hammer, a screwdriver and a saw. We tend to toss our tools about when a particular piece doesn't fit precisely. We throw our hands up in frustration, find the nearest person and declare, "You fix it!"

This attitude concerning instructions spills over into other areas. Locating a particular house, business or other landmark can become frustrating at times because we choose not to follow directions. We end up making excuses for our lack of geographical expertise.

I can handle instructions and directional signs like **DO NOT ENTER, LEFT LANE ENDS** and **AUTHORIZED PARKING ONLY: VIOLATORS WILL BE PROSECUTED.** They are short, sweet and to the point with a tendency to suggest a cause and affect situation.

Some of us simply assume directions. Recently, I offered to take off a reluctant radiator cap from Vic Morphew's car. As I was struggling to remove the cap, Carl, another fellow worker, approached the car. He watched intently and then made an observation pertaining to the small print on the cap.

"There's no need for those instructions," he said

slowly. I guess he was right. The small print read "turn slowly." The cap was so stubborn that that's about all I was able to do. Finally it came off.

I began the same straining process to replace the cap. Vic suggested that I turn the cap in the opposite direction this time. You know, the mechanical sage was right. Perhaps I should have read the small print after all.

Maybe we all need to read instructions, take our time, respect machinery and tools and proceed with caution when assembling anything. I'm trying. I am really trying. Amanda says I'm getting better about this.

I suppose I could make a very interesting model with all the left over parts I had from previous projects.

According to Murphy's law; there is never time to do it right the first time, but there is always time to do it over.

Sportswriting Is Violent

Sportswriters are a breed apart from news reporters. They provide readers with accounts of local, state and national sporting contests.

A sportswriter can dip a brush into a variety of colorful phrases to make broad strokes across the canvas of a sports page. Words used in their stories could be considered editorializing in the run-of-the-mill news reporting.

These writers are creative individuals within their own domain. They do not appear to be violent in nature. However, several of the sports they cover can be linked to violence, such as football, hockey and basketball.

Violent language to describe a grudge match between two rivals can be read in the following day's headlines: **Razorbacks demolish Longhorns 97-3.**

I love words. They can be used to describe an event, a feeling, or place with pinpoint accuracy, but everyday reporting should be "just the facts, ma'am. Just the facts."

For sportswriters, an artillery of verbs is at their disposal. Words like: bashed, slammed, crushed, ripped, slaughtered, hammered, crucified, rolled over, whips, slashes, murders, explodes, dumps, shoots down, thrashes, stomps, annihilates, beats, gunned down, tears apart and manhandled.

If I took the liberty of writing an article, say, of a city council meeting with the flair and vocabulary afforded a sportswriter, the account of that session in the next day's edition would read something like this:

Alderman Fred Swartz slammed a proposal presented by Mayor Harvey Hoots in Tuesday night's five-hour Beaverdale City Council meeting marathon.

"In your face," Swartz said.

A two hour discussion of the merits associated with providing dental floss for homeless canines by the city council was batted around the table.

Alderman Ruby Stutzburger manhandled City Attorney Claudell Huffman III because she believed he had gunned down her proposed plan to observe Canine Care Week to be scheduled for Feb. 25 – March 2.

Huffman annihilated Stutzburger's meager attempt to spend the city's nearly depleted budget.

Members of the audience were divided on the issue. In the heat of the moment, several participants began flinging accusations at the others in hopes of demolishing their proposals.

The session continued another two hours until 252 pound, Alderman Fredricka Bluebuns, hammered home her main concern, which was to paint tree trunks to match the nearest house.

The meeting was adjourned after Mayor Hoots called a delay penalty.

In reality, I believe readers would appreciate a bit more violence in news accounts of community gatherings. But alas, "just the facts."

Sportswriters have another side to their personality. They are also gentle, caring and passionate individuals who love what they do.

Every Tuesday, nationwide, these writers use the following words to describe the outcome of rival contests: nips, nudges, edges, surprises, subdues, upsets, squeaks by, embarrasses, pushes, slips past, suppresses, out-classes, flounders, cruises past, eases by and stings.

I admire sportswriters. Their flamboyant way with words produces a "like being there" feeling while reading their accounts of sporting events.

If I had a chance to write a real news story with a sportswriter's flair, I would probably be eliminated, ousted, ejected, flushed, dropped, destroyed, massacred, trampled, bombed, blitzed, battered and nuked.

I'll just stick to the facts for now.

1970 Class Reunion

The news finally came and it took just twenty years to arrive. Apparently, some members of the 1970 Arkansas High School graduating class decided our class needed to get together, so invitations were mailed. Mine was sent to my parent's address in Texarkana. I thought plans to celebrate this historic occasion had been placed on the back burner since no event was scheduled during the summer.

It seems three separate get-togethers are beginning to take shape for September. We are to meet at the football field where my Alma Mater hosts the Panthers of Benton High School.

A get-together-to-eat-talk-and-lie party is also planned. Several types of discussions will probably take place here. Old classmates talk about how successful they are among their peers. Another conversation includes the "Gee, you sure have lost a lot of weight since the last time I saw you." What people do not know is that each person has probably lost and gained about 100 pounds several times since 1970, not including the crash-diet fiasco before coming to this reunion.

I refuse to jump feet first into a diet for a 20 year high school reunion. I either like me the way I am or I don't.

(Although, I really need to lose about 30 pounds.)

What is it about "coming home" that most of us want to return as the conquering hero? Who do we need to impress? Why can't we be who we have become and call it even?

When I think about two of my close high school friends, Bill Wharton and Franz Baskett, I realize how much we have had in common over the past two decades. Our first marriages ended in divorce. However, each of us has since happily remarried.

Bill has a law practice in Little Rock. Franz, an artist and poet, lives in Fayetteville (but recently has accepted a teaching position at Ole Miss), and then there is me, a former minister turned reporter and columnist.

Our age has begun to manifest itself in a number of ways. Bill has the most gray hair, Franz has less hair and I have the longest.

Probably the best activity at this reunion will be reminiscing. For the first time since high school, we can be comfortable about what we did and thought during those "coming of age" years.

We will attempt to find out if some classmates were really prudish or just very smart. Was the smartest student at Arkansas High a genius or extremely sly with a cheat sheet. Perhaps even some "locker room" talk will be verified among the ranks.

I wonder if the class of 1970 will boast any former Savings and Loan or Housing and Urban Development officers? If so, their stories of crisis will undoubtedly take up conversation time.

"If there is a tragedy or a crisis of notable merit, there will always be an Arkansas connection" – Haley's Law: Article 3, Section 42 b.

No Cure for Waiting

Waiting.

We wait for something every day of every year.

On the long weekend after everything was created, God said, "Let there be waiting." Sure enough it happened. I guess most theologians would call it "Original Waiting."

God turned to Fred, the angel, and said, "That ought to keep them guessing for a while." Fred was picking his teeth as he leaned against a gold column at the Pearly Gates and said, "God, I was waiting for you to do that." So waiting began in the Garden.

Adam was growing very impatient. I think it had something to do with a contract to receive the knowledge of good and evil.

Eve gave Adam a gentle hug and said, "Why don't you eat this apple while you wait." A puzzled Adam asked, "What is a wait?"

She said, "I don't know. It just came to me after I finished eating this apple."

Statistics have shown that we spend approximately three years of our lives waiting.

We wait for coffee to brew, bread to toast, traffic lights to change, planes to catch and doctors; just to name a few.

People tell us when we should wait. Wait until you are at least 35 before you marry. Wait until you are financially able before you buy a house. Wait ... wait ... wait ...

I want to tell these people, who seem to have the wisdom of Solomon, a few things.

There is never a "good time" to get married. You fall in love, jump in and swim. You do it using the backstroke, the American crawl or by simply treading water.

There is never a "good time" to have babies. Isn't it amazing that the first question people ask a newlywed couple is, "When are you going to have a baby?" You just have them – either by intentional planning or by little surprises.

There is never a "good time" to buy a house, but it sure beats paying rent and watching those monthly checks fly away with nothing left to call your own. Thank God and financial lending institutions for 30 year loans.

There is never a good time to wait.

Some people watch television while they wait. Exercise seems to fill up the time for some, while reading occupies the moments for others.

My Dad has been waiting all his life. I've heard him say on many different occasions, "I'm waiting for my ship to come in!" As an adult, I know the only things that seem to come in are the tide and a few unwanted bills.

A wise sage once said, "Good things come to those who wait." He obviously never had to wait for any length of time. I would like to amend that statement to read, "Good things come to those who CAN wait."

I hate to wait.

We have woven "waiting" into our vocabulary. We tell others to: wait a second, wait a minute, wait on me. There is the ever-popular, "wait `till you father gets home!"

Children really can't wait either. The car is barely out of the driveway before one of the kids says, "How many more miles? What time is it? When will we get there?"

There is no known cure for waiting. It is a disease which goes back to the Garden.

I guess God had a reason for creating the animal called "waiting."

I'll just sit here, ponder, and wait for an answer. This is going to take a while. Do you have something you need to do?

Ahhh-Ahh Choo!

A whiff of black pepper, a speck of dust in the air, or ragweed particles can be the culprits that lead to – ah...ahh...ahhh choo! – a big sneeze.

Sneezes vary in their intensity. Some are petite and others sound like a thunder clap. We are forewarned of the impending blast from some, while others catch us off guard completely.

Amanda's sneeze is dainty, it hardly merits being called a sneeze. But I have heard her blow her nose on several occasions and it sounded like Gabriel blowing his trumpet.

Every person within earshot of my father's sneeze is warned by his false starts and near-sneezes. When he does sneeze, the needle bounces near 4.9 on the Richter scale. Not one, but as many as six sneezes are heard before the series ends.

According to the 1989 Guinness Book of World Records, the worst chronic sneezing fit ever recorded is that of Donna Griffiths (born 1969) of Pershore, England. She starting sneezing on Jan. 13, 1981, and surpassed the previous endurance record of 194 days on July 27, 1981. Griffiths sneezed an estimated one million times in the first 365 days. She achieved her first sneeze-free day on Sept.

16, 1983. It was the 987th day. (Note: the highest speed at which expelled particles have been measured to travel is 103.6 mph.)

Some folks use different sneeze techniques. These include holding the nose, which can be deadly on the eardrums; the closed mouth sneeze, which produces the bulged-eye look; and the no-holds-barred sneeze where the mouth is not closed, nor covered, and the nose is not held. It is just "let it all hang out."

I am confident that most of us have tried to prevent a sneeze by placing a finger underneath our nose. This procedure works only as long as we keep our finger there. Mostly, we cover our mouth and let it go.

Sneezes attack at the most inopportune moments. Some occur when we are involved in a serious activity: a funeral, a wedding, final tests, a golf match or other occasion. In each case, the possibility of a sneeze is dreadful. I hate to sneeze while driving down the interstate, it makes me run off the road.

The sneezing and burping combination can also put our body through all sorts of contortions.

The most absolute moment of terror strikes when I have just put a bite of food in my mouth and I realize a sneeze is approaching. Sometimes I make it to a napkin, other times I don't. This event occurs most often at breakfast. It may have something to do with pepper on my eggs.

"Gesundheit" is an expression of good wishes to someone who has just sneezed. Often we hear "God bless you" or perhaps the generic version – "bless you."

Sometimes life situations keep us from being suave, cool and "etiquettely" proper. These moments happen to all of us, young and old alike.

I suppose the only thing to do when a sneeze approaches is let it rip and allow our humanness to show. Be proud of your unique style of sneezing, but do apply manners.

Columnist Mistaken for Whale

My recent columns on jumbo cheeseburgers and Bubba pizzas have finally taken their toll on me. I really didn't set out to write so much about food. It just happened. You know – *food happens.*

On two different occasions, I managed to pop the top button on a pair of pants. A few extra pounds seems to have miraculously appeared around my waist.

It's time to get serious about losing a few pounds. All right, about 10. Okay, okay, about 20. Perhaps I could go up to 40, but that's my final limit.

I heard a comedian tell about a new style of jeans. He said jeans come in prewashed and prefaded. He suggested another style with prerolled waist bands for large folks like me.

Until I lose some weight, swimming may be hazardous to my health. I might be harpooned for a white whale. Just call me "Shamu."

A strict vow of "diet" was proclaimed. No type of tempting food was to be brought into the house. I made up my mind. I would give "them" a week and "they" could take off the weight. The first day I didn't eat anything until an afternoon apple.

Amanda arrived from work with her arms full of six boxes of Girl Scout cookies. She had forgotten about her earlier order.

I had a chicken pot pie on the table for our supper. Needless to say, our diet went out the window. A glass of milk and half a box of cookies began my desert.

The next morning, I had a glass of "Thin Quick" to start my diet again.

I wasn't at work 30 minutes, when my editor sent me on an errand of mercy. My mission was to purchase a dozen doughnuts.

I didn't eat a single one.

Later, our food editor invited me to represent *The Benton Courier* as a judge at a crawfish festival and gumbo cook-off contest.

I did not need to be led into temptation. I found the way on my own.

At lunch, I had another glass of "Thin Quick." That evening, Amanda walked through the door carrying a can of golden candy nuggets filled with peanut butter. It was another forgotten purchase.

After devouring a couple of tuna sandwiches, I grabbed a handful of nuggets for desert. I ate them like peanuts, two at a time, while watching a few television programs. The can emptied quickly. Oh well, I'll start again tomorrow.

The following morning, I forgot to gulp my "Thin Quick" drink. During my morning news assignments, I walked past Posey's 66 service station just to say "hello."

"Come on in and have a piece of lemon cake," James Posey said.

"No, thank you, I can't," I replied.

I ended up eating a big hunk of it anyway. Again, I didn't drink my lunch-in-a-glass.

Will power and stick-to-itness is more easily said than done.

Amanda and I purchased a stepping machine to simulate walking up a flight of stairs. I broke it one day at lunch after 56 steps.

Next, we bought a ski machine to exercise our arms and legs as cross-country skiing would do. She has exercised more with it than I have. I found another use for the machine; it makes a great place to hang my clothes after I iron them.

There is never a good time to diet no matter how much we want to. Maybe we need to follow the advice from the NIKE sports shoe commercials. **JUST DO IT.**

Race Brings Pride and Humility

I really enjoy running. Getting back into the daily practice of running is another thing. Several years ago I was running eight miles a day. Running around noon was good for me. There was a sense of accomplishment as I felt sweat pouring down my face and the heat from the sun on my neck. Close to the end of the run, all I could think about was a hot bath and Gatorade. Simple pleasures are the best.

Early on, embarrassment had kept me from entering any races. Who wants to be last? I didn't want an old man or woman to beat me. However, I managed to overcome this and decided to give it a try. My first race was a 5K race during Brickfest in Malvern. I was told by my friend, John Thomas (a marathon runner), that everyone gets the pre-race jitters.

As I scanned the already crowded starting line, I saw a very good representation of different walks of life.

I noticed 60-year-old men who looked like they were in remarkable physical shape, along with several very overweight men who, I thought, needed to be watching the race instead of participating. The race was highlighted with the young, slim, beautiful and handsome runners in their early twenties and thirties.

Then there were people like me.

All I wanted to do was finish this 3.1 mile race without the aid of the medical emergency team.

We looked liked cattle shuffling, spitting and stretching as we got ready for the starter's pistol to fire. (They had a shotgun in Malvern.) At the signal, the mass of runners exploded like a bullet from a rifle.

I became acutely aware that I couldn't take a deep breath. I came to the first milemarker and the man clocking our time said, "6:47," as I ran past him. No wonder I couldn't breathe! I was accustomed to running a ten-minute mile during the week. I paced myself and was doing all right until two women came beside me.

I thought to myself, "I'm not going to let these women outrun me." The macho mentality was coming out.

I would move ahead, then, they would. After shuffling positions several times, I was unable to take a deep breath. Finally, they kicked into overdrive and left me. I quickly realized a 5K race is no place for an inflated male ego mentality.

Once upon a time, I had this same mentality in other matters. I had the preconceived notion that all ministers should be men. This was before I entered seminary at Southern Methodist University in Dallas.

The late Beverly Sawyer, a very close friend and a United Methodist minister, was the one that broke this macho veil for me. She had a wonderful spirit about her. Gifts of writing, listening, caring, and love were only part of her priestly package.

She gently persuaded me to broaden my mind on the idea of women in the ministry, as well as other areas.

I quickly realized God moves in all circles. God can call men as well as women into the ordained ministry. This is something God has been doing for years.

Since 1979, I have observed how women in positions normally held by men are treated. I am not a raving women's libber. I only point things out and comment. There are women in all areas of the work place. We have women postmasters, executives in management, newspaper editors and a host of others.

Equal pay for equal work is not only fair, it's justice.

Let's face it, women can do anything men can do. Sometimes they do a better job. There is a small poster displayed on the door of an office in Benton. It reads: *They found something that does the work of five men – ONE WOMAN.* The "good ol' boys" in the South can't say they weren't warned.

I did finish that race in Malvern. My time was a respectable 22:43 and I wasn't last, only very tired.

Satchel Page once said," Don't look back, someone might be gaining on you."

I have quit looking back!

High School Reunion Survivor

Life has changed much during the past two decades. In 1970, the Vietnam War was in high gear and long hair was found only on "hippies."

Today, the country teeters on the edge of war in the Middle East and cowboys and old hippies alike have long hair. The rebels of the '60s and early '70s have emerged as the Establishment and heavyweight decisions are being made by them.

At our 20th high school reunion, members of the 1970 graduating class of Arkansas High School in Texarkana discussed many issues. We all agreed that we are survivors. We survived the hideous "Disco" phase without too many problems.

Life issues were identified in conversations. Our class had its share of second and third marriages. Age was a common factor in many chats.

Men who once sported flowing locks, now can wash and dry their hair with a wash cloth. Gray seemed to abound on a few heads, while a weight problem frustrated others.

My shoulder-length hair didn't surprise most of my friends. "You've always been a hippie," one classmate remarked.

A reunion dance brought out many classmates. I thought people would be dancing to the music of our era. Instead, I discovered people only wanted background music for talking and visiting. Some of the conversations at the dance were reminiscent of our parents. "I wonder if we can turn the music down," a classmate said.

Not everyone wanted to chitchat. A couple dressed in Western boots, blue jeans and black T-shirts burned up the dance floor with the Texas two-step. They came to party. Someone asked, "Do you know who he is? I think he graduated with us. I think his last name is Cornett."

Come to find out, Steve Cornett did graduate with us. He had put on a few pounds and was several inches taller than we remembered.

Alan Forrest, our class jester, stopped at my table and shared a life experience with me. It was a case of following your heart as a result of a career change.

He was making a good salary for an electronics firm in Texas. The company gave him an option – either move to California or lose your job. He did not want to go to California so he left his job.

Sitting at the table at home, he made a list of things he could do. Tennis always remained near the top. He is now teaching tennis in Grapevine, Texas, where he resides. Alan may not make as much money as before, but he is happy.

When conversation got around to age, some of it centered on health-conscious data. I joked with one classmate about not watching my cholesterol or putting more bran in my diet. "Because of this obsession with bran, before long we will be eating pulp wood for the roughage content," I said.

At Friday night's football game, Texarkana Razorbacks vs. Benton Panthers, Amanda, a graduate of Bryant High School, had promised she would yell for my alma mater. After four plays, she was standing up rooting for the Benton Panthers. I remained loyal to Texarkana.

"We could move to the Benton side at the half and still save this marriage," she said with a small chuckle.

The Texarkana Razorbacks won by a slim margin and my marriage continues to be strong.

What will our 25th high school reunion bring? Some of us will probably share our extensive photo collection of our grandchildren and comfort each other with the belief that life still begins at 40.

Quit the Griping

We can find them running around everywhere. No laws can protect us from their presence. They are in the office place, alongside us on assembly lines and at business counters. We find it difficult to work in an environment where we hear their steady drivel.

Who are these creatures? Whiners, complainers and gripers.

Some may not start out their day complaining, however, they are influenced by those around them. As the day wears on, they gradually transform into Super Complainer. Most of them are not content with their own lives so they inflict their dissatisfaction on the rest of us.

Nothing suits them. When it rains, they want sunshine. When it is warm, they want cold. If someone receives a compliment, they find ways to undermine it.

Life is unfair, they say. I agree. At times life is a bit uneven and ragged on the edges, but we learn to muddle through each day. Phrases like "It all comes out in the wash," "What goes around, comes around," and "I'll let God handle this one," seem to bring comfort when we feel our lives have been thrown off balance.

Just look around. We see folks who are in worse

situations then we could ever possibly find ourselves. We wouldn't trade our problems for theirs if our lives depended upon it.

Among the ancient pages of the Good Book, we find the story of a famous person who had every right to gripe and complain, but decided not to. His name: Job.

Job was the pawn in a chess match between God and the Devil. It seems that Job was an all right kind of guy. He crossed his t's and dotted his i's, attended Sabbath temple services, never used a harsh word toward another person, fathered a large family and worked hard to acquire plenty of money. He was well-respected about town and was beloved of God. Job was the model of contentment.

In this terrestrial chess match, the Devil made a deal with God saying, "I'll bet you eternity that I can make Old Job forget he ever knew you."

"Bring it on, fool," God said. "Gimme your best shot." So the Devil did. Job had no inkling of what was about to take place.

Little by little, livestock, sons, daughters and wealth were taken from him. Mrs. Job became very irritated and shouted those infamous words,"Curse God and die!" Still, Job kept quiet, endured his pain and remained faithful.

Gradually, disease (accompanied by sores and boils) infiltrated Job's body. He continued to accept these misfortunes and refused to blame God for his troubles. Job simply said, "The Lord giveth and the Lord taketh away." Some might think this suggests that God is an Indian giver.

Job's health, wealth and family were eventually returned to him. I wonder how happy he was to have another 20 years to listen to Mrs. Job? I don't know. Job never complained.

I am not an advocate for the eradication of complaining. At times there is a place for legitimate griping, especially when injustice or hurt is evident. But to wake up each morning with the sole purpose of whining (woe is me), complaining (life is unfair) or griping (I never get a break) is a tiring way to start a day.

Conserve energy. It really does take more energy to whine, complain and gripe than it does to be positive.

Wornout Shoes Remain Faithful

People keep everything. We hate to throw anything away. One never knows what an item will be worth in the years ahead.

One particular article that has been difficult for me to deliver to the garbage heap is a pair of wornout deck shoes. At the end of a workday, the first thing I slip my tired feet into are these comfortable, yet ugly shoes. They are badly scuffed and there is splattered evidence of past painting projects on the tops. The inner sole on the left shoe has loosened and needs a few drops of glue.

My feet feel so good when I have them on that I may never be able to part with them. I usually wear them around the house. However, I have been seen sporting them as I pursue shopping errands.

Some may say they have been beaten with an "ugly" stick, but to me they are beautiful because they feel so good.

Another article that seems to evade the dumpster is a pair of "holey" blue jeans. I'll bet these same-type jeans hang in closets all over America, despite the many threats from spouses to trash them.

Nothing can compare to a pair of personally wornout jeans. The jean manufacturers try to produce a prewashed, worn-out pair, but no matter how many times the jeans are bleached and washed at the plant, it cannot take the place of our old ones.

We have a deep respect and long-lasting relationship with them. Those new, stiff jeans are a challenge to us. Finally, after years of wear and hours of washing, they are perfect.

A popular trend seems to be a pair of "shotgun-blasted" jeans. The price tag is as large as one of the many holes. A pair of these would make a nice Christmas present for that discriminating person on your list. How ironic. We never dreamed our ragged jeans could be such a trend setter.

How can we part with close friends like these old clothes? The only way would be to gain so much weight that it deters our pulling them on our bodies. (I hesitated to say this.)

I have saved some "perfect" jeans, although I would need to grease my ankles to get them on. After I struggled to button them, I would pray (as Amanda has said) there would be no internal injuries during the day.

Another worn-out item of worth may be a pair of ragged house slippers. The old ones feel so much better than the new ones. The bath robe could also be a treasure. You know the one. It looks as if it has been a shepherd's costume in a thousand Christmas pageants. Stuck all the way in the back of the closet, this robe has a permanent place among the rest of our clothes. It shall remain there because of sentimental value.

Some things are beautiful because they feel comfortable. We believe we can make it through another hectic day or perhaps a stressful life knowing some things remain constant.

I wonder if friends could be considered in this light. Old friends are priceless treasures that remain with us.

Feathers Ruffled by Buzzards

According to a modern day sage, it's difficult to fly like an eagle when one is surrounded by so many turkeys. This time it's not the turkeys that are giving me problems.

There seems to be two despicable buzzards often circling above our heads just waiting to nest in our hair. Their names are negativity and judgment.

These feathered fowls of failure can be spotted flying around the workplace, perched in the house, or anywhere people are gathered.

I was recently made aware of these creatures during some conversations with several friends. One of the main complaints stemmed from the outbursts of negative people in an office.

Negativity and judgment seem to go hand in hand, I told my friend. At least that is what Dr. Wayne Dyer believes in his book, *You'll Believe It When You See It.*

A person who is critical and judgmental exposes more about himself than about the person who receives the brunt of his banishment.

When I was a parish minister, I heard a multitude of complaints ranging from the order of the worship service to the lack of food prepared by parishioners and brought to a church potluck.

A few selected phrases also used by church members were: "We've never done it this way before"... "We tried that a few years ago and it didn't work"... "It won't work, preacher!"... "We're not ready for this yet."

Hope emerges from positive people with positive thoughts, while hopelessness thrives in negativity.

Once we know ourselves and like the people we have become, it really doesn't matter too much what the negative numbskulls say. We learn to let their comments roll like water off a duck's back.

Negative naggers appear to be very unhappy creatures. Happiness must have eluded them at some point in their lives.

Under a constant flame of negativity, happiness can evaporate. I know we can't always see the positive side to many of our situations but, perhaps, we can refuse to submit to negativity all the time.

Excuse me. I'll talk with you at another time. My shotgun is loaded and I am ready to shoot a few buzzards circling my head.

Wasteful Worry Saps Our Vigor

Some of us dangle on the edge of developing ulcers, irritating rashes and a mixture of other symptoms due to our worrying about a medley of situations. I worry, but then I try to let it go. Sometimes, I'm even successful at it.

The broad smiling face of Alfred E. Newman, pictured on the cover of the famous MAD magazine gave the world his philosophy on worry. It was this: "What? Me Worry?"

There are many worry warts who do not subscribe to Newman's thought. These folks believe life is not worth living unless one worries.

Wart people, in order to calm down, may purchase a string of "worry" beads to fiddle with.

Experts tell us that 40 percent of our worries never happen, 30 percent are about things that have already happened, 12 percent are needless worries about our health and 10 percent are about the petty things that don't amount to a hill of beans.

This adds up to 92 percent of our time. What this tells us is that out of 100 things we worry about, only eight are worth our concentration.

In 1986, the late Bob Gannaway of Little Rock had a

little book published entitled *Bumble Bees Can't Fly (But they do. And so can you.)*

Gannaway remembered the day a grade school teacher told him that judging by the size of its body and wings, and the principles of science, bumble bees are not supposed to be able to fly. I discovered all the necessary tools to fly between the pages of Gannaway's 85-page book.

Excessive worry clips our wings and prevents us from taking off in flight. The following story of a worrier was told by Gannaway in his book:

One night a man from Pine Bluff, Arkansas, was awakened by a severe pain in his side. He reached under the covers and felt a large knot. He was shaken, but decided to ignore it, hoping it would go away.

That didn't work. When he awoke the next morning it was still there. The knot apparently had grown. The man decided to try a different approach.

He would not shower but would just dress and go to work without looking. Again – failure.

That night, when he felt the lump, it was larger and much more tender. He decided he had no other choice except to face the awful truth. The man loosened his belt, turned down his pants, and found a big . . . tick.

He had spent a sleepless night and a nonproductive day worrying about his health.

I have no easy answers to offer on how to stop

worrying. However, the percentages are good that you and I can choose the important things to worry about and let go of the wasteful worries.

Now. Don't you feel a bit lighter? Perhaps even light enough to fly.

A Fashion 'Faux Pas' Unveiled

My day began like any normal working day, waking up early enough to gulp down two cups of coffee, press a shirt and a pair of slacks, shower and then venture out into a new morning. Sometimes normal days are laced with little surprises. This was one of them.

I made one stop on my way to work. I needed gas for my truck. When I got out and attempted to fill up my tank, it was on the other side. I had pulled up on the wrong side of the pump.

With everything corrected and fuel pumping furiously, I looked down to notice there was a black loafer on my left foot and a brown one on my right. Probably no one noticed, but I felt like I was wearing a pair of Bozo-the-Clown shoes. Embarrassed, I hurriedly finished my chore and walked inside to pay. The smiling cashier asked me, "How's it going?"

"Well, from the ankle up, everything is just fine," I said. Then I told her my shoe problem. (Come to think about it, I had another pair just like them at home.)

This day, December 7, happened to be the 49th anniversary of the Japanese attack on Pearl Harbor. I felt as if a bomb had been dropped at my feet.

I rushed back to the house to find Amanda ironing a sweater. I just stood there. "What's wrong with this picture?" I asked. She covered her mouth to conceal a factitious grin.

I trudged to the closet and realized what went haywire. My problem was not that I was color-blind; it was the fact that I did not turn on the light that would have allowed me to locate a pair of matching shoes.

My shoes are in a rack on the closet floor. I simply reached down, felt around in the dark, and grabbed a pair of loafers.

My morning "faux pas" was shared with friends throughout the day. We might as well laugh at ourselves and beat others to it.

Rarely do I take the time to switch on a room light when making a midnight run to the refrigerator. Occasionally, I end up bumping a chair leg with my little toe. Then, and only then, do I consider turning on a light.

A Christmas-kind-of thought came to mind about the third time I told the story. Our days can become dull and dim by running errands, working long hours, cooking meals, attending meetings and a host of other daily chores. Perhaps this season we will not stumble in the darkness we have created. During this Christmas season, maybe we can gather with loved ones to celebrate the light which promises to break through our darkness.

From now on let's just leave the light on.

Running Away in Small Circles

When we think of runaways, our mind's eye pictures a scenario of a wayward youth who feels misunderstood and decides to leave his surroundings for greener fields. However, the fertile pastures become dark city streets with unfamiliar faces.

Who hasn't thought of running away? The mother, who is president of various committees carrying loads of responsibility, may dream of riding into the sunset and leaving worries and cares behind when her housework piles up. Perhaps the hard working businessman, who tries to keep on top of things by doing more office work at home, daydreams of a place far away from communication devices and deadlines.

I ran away from home as a child. The reason for leaving is only a vapor trail of memory. The trip was cut short by a cloudburst followed by a downpour the same night.

Packed neatly in a red bandanna were my worldly possessions: a peanut butter and jelly sandwich, 21 baseball cards, a pocket knife and three *Sgt. Rock* comic books. After securing my belongings onto a stick, I announced to my parents, "I'm leaving and I'm not coming back."

Being a parent myself, I believe my parents were caught somewhere between a laugh and a tear. They were laughing because they had heard the weather report, but they were crying inside because I meant what I had said.

I traveled around the block several times just to let them know I meant business. It didn't matter that I really wasn't going anywhere, I proved my point. I made my grand entrance. Well, it wasn't that grand. It was more like a prodigal son coming home.

My reappearance (I was wet from head to toe) proved a point to my parents, but I can't remember exactly what that point was. The passage of time has made the rest of the story a bit vague. However, I do remember feelings.

My anger had spilled all over the floor in small puddles, but a cozy embrace reassured me that I was loved. Mother made me dry and warm.

Soon I felt calm and relaxed. My soft pillow and cool sheets lulled me to sleep. All was right with the world once again.

Like the prodigal son, I was running away from myself. We can't escape ourselves no matter how hard we try. We simply travel around the block several times just to prove we're serious and return home. Facing others is the easy part. The difficult part lies hidden – facing ourselves.

My father tells the World War II story of the time he was responsible for guarding about 85 German prisoners during his stint in the Army. This gentle, humorous man from Tennessee made friends with at least half of the captives. Stationed in a guard tower equipped with a machine gun was not his favorite job. Eating in the mess hall was far more enjoyable than guarding prisoners.

One night, two prisoners escaped. They couldn't be found. After a couple of days the prisoners returned of their own free will. Why? They were hungry.

At times we are hungry and ready to ride into the sunset (or at least around the block). After a few lonely minutes, we click our heels and say, "There's no place like home. There's no place like home."

Mondays Deserve More Respect

Thank God Mondays come around only once a week.

Over the years, this infamous day has been the brunt of many harsh comments about its position on our calendars.

The day has been belittled by several songwriters. Such verses include, "Rainy days and Mondays always get me down," by the late Karen Carpenter of the Carpenters and "Monday, Monday, can't trust that day," bellowed by the Mammas and the Pappas during the mid-sixties.

"Well, it's old blue Monday," Benton weather watcher, Mary Etta Burks, observes as she provides weekend weather reports on Monday.

We usually start diets on Mondays, new jobs on Mondays, vacations on Mondays, celebrate federal holidays on Mondays and some service repairmen tell us they will get to it first thing Monday morning.

Monday is important to me as a writer because this column is published on that day. At times, this is the day whose shadow drifts across my shoulders and shows me another life observation of which to write about.

If it weren't for Monday, we wouldn't have Tuesday or the weekend. So, why does Monday always get a bad rap? Monday didn't do anything to us. Monday should get better treatment from us.

Mondays once gave me the nervous twitch when I was in public school. I was like 98.2 percent of the nation's students. Sunday evening was spent cramming homework that I had conveniently put off doing all weekend.

Why must students have homework on the weekends? A student's mother asked me that same question. This conversation centered around whether her school-age son had gotten his homework finished for Monday's classes. This was Sunday night.

Her argument, a convincing one, was that weekends were a time for families to spend together. She even suggested that school should be more like a job. Students would work Monday through Friday and be off on the weekends.

Perhaps we could give Congress a suggestion to change Monday's name to Funday. In reality, a name change wouldn't alter a thing. Monday begins our week and we have the power to decide what kind of day it will be.

Monday could be a fun day if all procrastinators would do what needed to be done at the appropriate time, if all fearful people could understand they have power over their fear, if all dieters would eat sensibly on weekends and if we made sure we were more prepared for new jobs and new projects.

No matter how good or bad Mondays are, we must go through them to get to the weekends. I hope this Monday has been good for you. If not, hold on, Friday is coming!

Goodness Is Hard to Pin Down

A relative of mine wore a button during the Christmas season which read, "Oh hell, I forgot to be good!" This seemed very appropriate for the time of year. In fact, if I had seen it in the store, I would have purchased one and displayed it proudly on my red Christmas sweater.

Good is what we hope to become, not necessarily what we are at the present time.

I believe there is good in the worst of people and bad in the best of people. Then we have you and me.

In our weaker and angrier times, we have said things we wish had never dripped from our lips. How many of us have wanted to retrieve words, spoken at untimely and inappropriate moments, and it was like reeling in a 12-pound catfish?

" ... of a favorable character or tendency and ... praiseworthy character," is what Mr. Webster says in defining "good".

Early in our lives, we learn the rewards for being good. If we are good little boys and girls, Santa will bring us presents. If we are bad, he brings us a stocking full of switches. It is so difficult for a child to be good for a whole year, let alone a 36-year-old kid.

"Be good" is sometimes heard when we leave a company of friends. Then they might add, "If you can't be good, be careful."

When describing a "good" person, we often compare them with others. Here are some examples:

* She never complains.
* He never gets angry.
* She never uses profanity.
* He only thinks of others, never himself.
* She always goes to church.
* He doesn't drink.
* She never says anything bad about anyone.
* She never gossips about others.
* He always plays by the rules.
* She never gambles.

This is only a partial list of the many characteristics people use to compare themselves with others who appear to be good.

If applied to us, how many of these would make us good? NONE OF THESE. Not doing something doesn't make a person good. If a person doesn't do a particular thing for fear of losing public acceptance, rather than sticking with their own convictions, what good is this?

Good people are everywhere. The sad part is that some do not think of themselves as good. Maybe most of their lives they have heard parents, relatives or others constantly bombard them with you're-no-good bombs. It is sad but true; some believe what they have heard and they carry the scars from these explosions deep inside.

Goodness comes from the heart. It has no social or economic distinction.

Let's be real. We are not going to be good all the time. Perfect is not our middle name. We make mistakes. We fall. We get up. We dust off the seat of our pants. We stand. We carry on.

Our hearts are the great indicators. Our hearts make us "good." We make it because we believe in ourselves and our principals, not in what others believe about us. They don't know our hearts.

Hand Cream is 'Udderly' Great

Even though products are designed and marketed for one purpose, a few folks find other uses for them.

Amanda recently told me of a purchase she was about to make. Four products were discussed, all of which had to do with animals – farm animals.

At first, I was a bit taken aback by the thought of using Mane'n Tail, a hair care product one could buy at a feed store. "Several women at work have used it with wonderful results," she assured me.

Before I responded, I checked it out with Keelee. She is the girlfriend of Nathan, Amanda's son. Much to my surprise, she used the product and raved about it. Keelee has long flowing locks that always look perfect. I figured that if the stuff helped her hair, it would not hurt mine. (Just a note. Keelee is on the verge of a modeling career in New York.)

Another product called Bag Balm, normally used on cow's udders, works great to keep dry hands moisturized. The product comes in an attractive red and green tin box, another feed store product. I took Amanda's word for it this time. When I rubbed some in my hands, I saw a cow's udders.

Bova Cream (as in Bovine cattle) was another purchase. This product keeps hands and teets from being chapped. It was something Jergen's may not be able to brag about.

The last one was a product called Hoofmaker. This product is used on cattle hoofs and is excellent for a person's fingernails. After using all these products, I almost began singing the childhood song about a farmer named McDonald.

I also learned about a few more products. Barbasol shaving cream, in the tube, is also a preventative for chapped hands. WD 40, a lubricant designed for squeaky hinges, has been sprayed on arthritic joints.

Amanda told me of a facial mask made with cucumbers and avocados. I've always known that lemon juice would lighten hair in the summer months and beer shampoos can be used to add protein to lifeless hair.

Milk baths are myths. Besides you would have every cat within three miles hovering over your bathtub.

We are ingenious creatures. When one product produces an effective result, we try using it in other ways.

This is an example of the free enterprise system, which leads me to my pet peeve. The marketing department of any successful product will occasionally come out with the "new and improved" version. I have yet to discover any real difference.

As far as using animal products, go ahead, take a walk on the wild side. It may be better than those designed for us. We are all God's creatures.

My First Mortality Checkup

I had an opportunity recently to participate in what is commonly referred to as a stress test. I do not suffer from an uncontrollable amount of stress, but I wanted to see how the old pumper was holding up after almost four decades of faithful service.

I felt a bit nervous at first, which caused my blood pressure to be somewhat high, but I was more relaxed after Judy Lyman, a cardiac nurse at Saline Memorial Hospital, assured me that everything would be all right.

I was ready to face my voluntary ordeal. First, I changed into a pair of gym shorts and running shoes. Photographs of my heart were taken through the miracle of an ultrasound machine. Next, I was hooked up to a computer and heart monitor.

I laughed as I approached the treadmill. A vision of a hilarious Bill Cosby Show segment flashed in my mind. Cosby's character, Dr. Heathcliff Huxtable, wanted to prove he was in great physical condition. He decided to indulge himself in a stress test, which proved to be more difficult than he had anticipated.

I mentioned to Dr. Bill Thomas that I would be 39 years old in October. "Most men come in to have their mortality checked around that age," he said.

Amanda and I walk two miles a day, at least three times a week. I felt confident that I could conquer this treadmill.

It was a light walk at first, but then the speed increased and the elevation began to rise. By the time my session had ended, I was running uphill.

I thought I could have continued, but that was all in my head. (My body thought differently.) It realized that I had made it.

It was time for another photo session of my heart. The pictures showed no leaks, the blood was pumping at a good steady rate of speed, and it was beating in a good geometrical shape, according to the reports and comments from Dr. Thomas.

Although I was pleasantly surprised with the test, there is still the obvious weight loss needed and my cholesterol level needs to be checked, also. With all things considered, it appears that I can look forward to a long life.

Heart problems are not always physical. Some are related to the way we feel in our heart of hearts. There are a variety of symptoms going around these days.

When we experience sadness, this condition is referred to as having a "heavy" heart. When we are in love, it causes hearts to "flutter."

Too much emotional pain can "break" our hearts. In

most cases, decisions need to be made by "following" our hearts. When we tell another person how really sincere we are, it is "heart-felt" or from the "bottom of our hearts."

The person we are in love with is our "sweetheart." We refer to the center of an issue as "the heart of the matter."

A person who doesn't like another person has a "cold" heart, or one who shows no emotion has a "hard" heart.

Perhaps we really need to pay attention to the condition of our hearts. This is where all our secret desires are kept. Life springs from our hearts.

There are instances when I allow my head to interfere with my heart. This simple act causes me to occasionally miss out on a special "heart" moment.

Treadmills and low-fat diets are of no help when it comes to these conditions. Perhaps what we need is a little more practice at listening to our hearts.

Change Is Scary, But Good

Change.

The very sound causes us to step back and take a deep breath. It's one of those words that causes our hearts to beat irregularly, beads of sweat to pop out on our foreheads and the palms of our hands to be cold and filled with perspiration.

However, each one of us will be faced with some sort of change that comes in many different situations and circumstances. As a long lost friend returning for a visit or as that persistent thorn in the flesh, change comes.

Are we really ever ready for this constant companion? What are the signs of this ever-present foe among our daily schedules?

There are no clues, only hunches. Change can occur when we least expect it. In my short time on this planet, I have gone through a number of different changes. Some have been very good and exciting, while others have come as tidal waves across my life. But, one does learn to roll with the punches.

Courage is a major factor in changing. There is always a certain amount of fear in the unknown. Once we are determined to face any situation head on, we will be able to deal with life and all that it pushes, throws or even dumps on us.

We are all in the middle of a tightrope, walking through life with one hand holding onto the past for security and the other reaching for the future with hope and faith.

In 1988, I changed careers after devoting 10 years to the United Methodist ministry. This change has been refreshing, exciting and pleasant.

There are times when we must, above all else, be true to our hearts and take a risk. If we do not take that chance, we might be stuck in a rut for years and have no one to blame but ourselves.

We rarely ever notice the changing of the leaves until, in a quiet moment, our eyes catch a glimpse of the beautiful colors. Real change is a gradual process. At times, we are so close to it, yet we cannot see any difference. Suddenly, we emerge as a different person with new ideas, new thoughts, new visions and a new attitude about life. When did this change happen?

Change goes hand in hand with making decisions. It's up to you and me to determine our own personal outcome. We decide for ourselves. We change by ourselves. We all have the power within.

Hey, did you see that leaf change over there?

Who Is Frances Rose Shore?

Some of us have had encounters with an ordinary person who later became a movie star, a famous singer or a star sports figure.

I will share a story that I heard often as a child. (As you read these lines, my father is probably telling this same story to a woman standing behind him in the grocery store express lane.)

My father attended the Kansas City Conservatory of Music and Art. While a student there, he met a Jewish girl named Frances Rose Shore from Winchester, Tennessee. At that time, she was studying voice at Vanderbilt University.

Occasionally, a group of students would enjoy conversation over cokes at a local drug store. It was during these gatherings that Dad struck up a friendship with this soon to be extraordinary singer.

Shore worked as a singer at a Nashville night club called The Wagon Wheel while she continued her voice lessons. Those singing lessons paid off. One day Frances Rose Shore got her long-awaited break from radio star Eddie Cantor.

Dad recalls the day, some years later, when he picked up a radio guide that carried this headline, "Dinah Shore

Makes Big Hit in New York."

The name Shore rang a bell. But could it be the same one? Just before he entered the Army he wrote to her. "She sent an autographed 'glamour' picture to me. That was in 1942," Dad said.

He told me he always thought she was "going to make it big" in the entertainment world. Dad had shared the same dream. "We studied with the same teacher," he recalls. "She is five years younger than I am."

A special place was made for Shore's photo in the Army Recreation Room. When Dad was discharged, he made a final trip to the Recreation room to retrieve his picture. His heart sunk. "Somebody took it," he said.

Dinah Shore continued her successful singing career and starred in a few movies. "She had a marvelous personality," Dad recalls.

She had left for Hollywood and my father taught music for a brief time in a Missouri county school. (That's another experience.)

Through the years, he saved Dinah's letters and another autographed picture. She has had a long and eventful career which she still enjoys today.

My father kept those same letters for years. I remember looking at them as he told this story.

On one occasion, my father discovered the box full of letters had been invaded by termites. Most of the letters and pictures were destroyed.

Dad wrote to her and described the fire that had almost destroyed our home and which, indeed, had caused her letters and photos to go up in flames. He asked for another signed picture to replace the one that had been destroyed. (He did not want to confess to her that we had termites.)

Dad received a replacement picture. His comments made about this picture were different from the observations made about the first one.

"She must have had a face-lift because she is as old as I am," Dad would say. I think Dinah Shore really does wear her age well. It must be all that "Holly Farms" Southern-fried chicken.

Dad told me he is happy to be singing at his age or doing anything at his age for that matter. My father will celebrate his 79th birthday in April.

If it is any consolation, Dad, you do not look like a 79-year-old and you do not sing like one either. Maybe you and Dinah have more in common than you ever realized.

(Note: My father continues to tell folks in Texarkana that he hugged Susan Dunn, Metropolitan Opera star from Saline County, at a benefit concert in Benton. Perhaps he can write to Susan for an autographed photo to add to his collection.)

Rainbow Sends Word to Soldier

I have an Operation Desert Storm story to tell. Stories from returning soldiers continue to be shared with family, friends and the news media.

Desert Rainbow is a county-wide support group of family and friends of those who served in the Persian Gulf War. At the organizational meeting, a name for the group was on the agenda. There were many such support groups already established.

The words "Desert Rainbow" popped in my mind. I offered the name as a possibility. When the name rolled out, so did the reason. "Since we are in Operation Desert Storm, we should be Operation Desert Rainbow because there is a rainbow after every storm," I told the group. It was adopted.

The rainbow has been a symbol of hope for me since the first time I had the story of Noah's Ark read to me as a child.

A very dear friend of ours from Little Rock told us her son was stationed near Kuwait. We would hear update reports about her son when he called or wrote home.

We told her of Operation Desert Rainbow and gave her a Desert Rainbow button. She liked the rainbow's symbol of hope and wanted to send one to her son.

Communications and mail were cut off before the package could be mailed. The fighting continued. Prayers for protection were offered.

Soon after his return, his mother finally had a chance to give him the rainbow button. He shared a beautiful story of a rainbow with her.

Life was rough living in a foxhole outside Kuwait for 100 days with only a tarp to cover his head.

He said it had rained "black, oily rain" every Sunday. On one particular Sunday, however, the rain stopped. He looked up and noticed the dark clouds separating and for the first time, a beautiful rainbow was painted across the sky.

At that point, he felt God's hand was working in his situation. His faith and his sense of humor had kept him going during those uncertain days, his mother said. He had felt the prayers of protection offered by family and friends.

A brief time passed before he realized what the rainbow's presence meant.

As he looked deep into his mother's eyes, he told her that shortly after observing the rainbow, they were notified that a cease fire had been called. It was truly a mother-and-child reunion as tears of joy welled up in their eyes. The rainbow touched her son in a very significant way.

Each time I tell this story I get "goose bumps" all over, as do those who hear it. Questions emerge.

You may ask yourself if this incident was just a coincidence or were there connections between the Old Testament symbol of a rainbow, the Persian Gulf rainbow and Operation Desert Rainbow?

Whether or not you believe God intervened and spoke through this symbol, the fact remains that it did happen.

I believe there will always be a rainbow for us after every storm we may face.

Tom Haley, an award-winning columnist, has been a reporter, staff writer and columnist for *The Benton Courier* since 1988. He and his wife, Amanda, reside in Benton with two cats and three dogs.